How to deal with death and probate

If you want to know . . .

How to Spend the Kid's Inheritance

All you need to know to manage a successful retirement

How to Earn Money in Retirement

Draw on a lifetime of experience to supplement your pension and stay in touch

Dealing with Death, Funerals, Wills and Bereavement

A paractical guide to what to do when someone dies

Making Your Own Will

howtobooks

For full details, please send for a free copy of the latest catalogue to:

How To Books
3 Newtec Place, Magdalen Road
Oxford OX4 1RE, United Kingdom
info@howtobooks.co.uk
www.howtobooks.co.uk

GORDON BOWLEY LLB

How to deal with death and probate

A SELF-HELP GUIDE

howtobooks

Published by How To Books Ltd,
3 Newtec Place, Magdalen Road,
Oxford OX4 1RE. United Kingdom.
Tel: (01865) 793806. Fax: (01865) 248780.
email: info@howtobooks.co.uk
www.howtobooks.co.uk

First edition 2003
Second edition 2006

British Library Cataloguing in Publication Data
A catalogue record for this book is available from
the British Library

Produced for How To Books by Deer Park Productions
Cover design by Baseline Arts Ltd, Oxford
Typeset by TW Typesetting, Plymouth, Devon
Printed and bound by Bell & Bain Ltd, Glasgow

NOTE: The material contained in this book is set out in good faith for
general guidance and no liability can be accepted for loss or expense
incurred as a result of relying in particular circumstances on statements
made in the book which is bought and sold on that basis. Laws and
regulations are complex and liable to change, and readers should check the
current position with the relevant authorities before making personal
arrangements.

Contents

Preface

For over thirty years I practised as a family solicitor and was much engaged in the fields of probate and wills. It became obvious to me that the majority of the cases I handled in these fields could have been dealt with by any reasonably intelligent layperson who had time available and a little professional guidance. In fact, in many solicitors' offices, executives and their assistants do much of the work involved in dealing with the estates of those who die. Of course there are other cases which require a great deal of legal knowledge and training, but these are the exceptional ones.

Sometime after retirement, I decided to write out for my wife Margaret and my son John, a step-by-step guide to the procedures to follow and the information that would be required to wind up my affairs when I die, without the necessity for professional help. Those writings became this work and I dedicate it to them as a token of my appreciation of the kindness and devotion that they have shown to me. I hope that both they and you will find it of use and a great moneysaver!

This book is not intended to deal with every eventuality, but I believe it will cover what needs to be known in the majority of 'ordinary' cases. It does not deal with the calculation of inheritance tax, but if you decide to deal with the estate yourself rather than employ a solicitor, the Personal Applications Section of the Probate Registry will arrange for the tax to be worked out for you. No attempt has been made to cover estates involving life interests in great detail, but throughout I have indicated where I consider professional assistance should be invoked. When deciding whether to deal with an estate yourself rather than hand it over to a solicitor, bear in mind that if you get stuck, you can always seek legal advice on a specific point or instruct a solicitor to handle a particular stage – for example, you might wish to write all the letters and only ask the solicitor to prepare and lodge the probate forms. Such a course would reduce the cost considerably and I have included suitable specimen letters with relevant addresses in the appendices.

In spite of its limitations, I honestly think that this book includes all that it is necessary to know to enable the intelligent novice, with the necessary time available, to wind up most estates in England or Wales.

Go to it and good luck!

Author's notes

◆ This book only deals with the law applicable to England and Wales. Scottish law is different. Moreover, law and practice do change frequently and while every effort has been made to ensure that the contents of this short work are accurate and up to date, no responsibility is accepted for any loss resulting from acting, or from failure to act, as a result of it and the book is bought and sold on that basis.

◆ Throughout the book, for simplicity's sake and not for any reasons of gender prejudice, I have assumed that the usual case of the male of the species predeceasing the female will occur and 'he' should be read as 'she' or 'they' where the context and circumstances so require.

◆ The Department for Work and Pensions and the administration of Social Security Benefits were reorganised in April 2002.

Benefits for people of pensionable age will be dealt with in the future by the new Pensions Service and benefits for those of working age will be dealt with by the Employment Service operating from the Job Centre.

Claims for benefit from the Social Fund will be dealt with by the Employment Service offices irrespective of the age of the claimant.

Because these changes are being rolled out gradually over different parts of the country it is not possible to generalise and state which arrangements will be in force in any particular part of the country at any particular time. Accordingly when reading this book it might be necessary to construe references to the Benefits Agency as references to the Pensions Service or to the Employment Service.

◆ Crown copyright is acknowledged in respect of all statutory and governmental material quoted or referred to in the text.

Part 1

How to Proceed
on a Death

(1)

Dying

DEATH

Most people die naturally as the result of organ failure or disease; others suffer accidental deaths and yet others die as the result of the action or inaction of themselves or of others. Modern developments in medicine have given us the opportunity to control the time and manner of our dying to an extent which would have been unimaginable to our grandparents, and these developments have also inevitably thrown up hitherto undreamt of legal, sociological and philosophical problems. Indeed, modern medical developments have blurred the distinction between life and death. For our grandparents death occurred when the heart ceased to beat and the lungs to breathe, but today heartbeat, breathing and body nourishment can be artificially sustained even after the brain has died. Is a person in such a condition alive or dead?

There is little of extraordinary note to be said about the legal aspects of dying naturally after one's allotted span. When interference with the course of nature occurs, the legal consequences for all concerned differ considerably according to the circumstances of each case and what form of interference takes place, and there is the question of whether or not the interference should or should not take place. This book is not intended to cover sociological or philosophical matters. It is intended to be a brief practical guide to point the layman along the road to what he can, cannot and should do and indicate how he might do it.

CAN ONE CHOOSE THE TIME OR MANNER OF ONE'S DEATH?

Until the passing of the 1961 Suicide Act suicide and attempted suicide were criminal offences in the United Kingdom, although there was not much that could be done about it if it was successful. Today suicide is no longer a criminal offence, but life insurance policies will not pay out in such cases.

Although suicide is not a criminal offence, assisting suicide is. The Director of Public Prosecutions may seek the imprisonment for up to 14 years of anyone who aids, abets, counsels or procures the suicide of another or an attempt by another to commit suicide. No matter how heart-rending the circumstances, euthanasia (sometimes called mercy killing) is also illegal and because of the rule that no one can profit financially from their own crime, anyone who engages in mercy killing not only risks imprisonment but will be unable to inherit from the deceased's estate.

The positive act of killing without the deceased's consent is, of course, always illegal under English law, but there is generally no obligation to act to attempt to save a life unless one has expressly or impliedly undertaken such an obligation, as in the case of, for example, a doctor in relation to his patient. If the obligation has been undertaken it cannot legally be shed without the proper consent of the person in respect of whom it has been undertaken, unless one makes arrangements for another to undertake it. For a doctor to withdraw treatment with the patient's consent is not a criminal or a civil offence, but there is a distinction between treatment and basic nursing care designed to make the patient as comfortable as possible, such as washing. Basic nursing care cannot be withdrawn, even with the patient's consent.

In cases of terminal illness there is sometimes a narrow distinction between homicide or assisting suicide and the withdrawal of medical treatment; the one involves the introduction of an external element which causes death and the other allows causes which are already present in the body to cause death. In cases of doubt the guidance of a court can be sought in advance.

It is a principle of English law that, as one judge has put it, 'a mentally competent patient has an absolute right to consent or refuse consent to medical treatment for any reason, rational or irrational, or for no reason at all, even where that decision may lead to his or her own death'. A person is presumed to be mentally competent to take the decision and the onus of proving a lack of mental capacity is on those who claim that the capacity does not exist. As the same judge has said, 'A person lacks capacity if some impairment or disturbance of mental functioning renders the person unable to make a decision whether to consent to or refuse treatment'.

The question is not one of the right to self-determination but what is in the patient's best interest, looked at subjectively from the patient's point of view, and if the patient is competent, he is the person who is entitled to decide the question. For others, such as doctors, to override the patient's wishes is 'benevolent paternalism' and an assault. For this reason, although there will be no relevant Act of Parliament until the Mental Capacity Act 2005 is eventually brought into force (probably in April 2007), the Common Law recognises living wills or advance directives as they are sometimes called.

LIVING WILLS

A living will, sometimes called an advance directive, is a document which is made by a mentally competent person aged 18 or over and which sets out what medical treatment that person wishes, or does not wish, to undergo in specified circumstances. Living wills are useful in that they may be relied upon if at a future date the maker loses the powers of making decisions or communication, e.g. as a result of falling into a coma or suffering a stroke. They can assist relatives and doctors to achieve the correct decision and save them from much worry about what the patient would wish when agonising decisions have to be made.

To be valid a living will must state the maker's true wishes and accordingly it must be made voluntarily, without pressure, influence or encouragement by another person. It must be made by a person who has the required mental capacity. A person has sufficient mental capacity to make a living will if he is fully aware of the relevant circumstances, treatments and their implications and can:

◆ understand the relevant information;

◆ retain the relevant information;

◆ weigh the relevant information in the balance so as to arrive at a proper choice; and

◆ communicate the decision made.

The person making the will must not be rendered mentally incapable of reaching a balanced judgement when the will is made by reason of illness, mental distress or anything else. A person is presumed to be mentally competent to take the decision and the onus of proving a lack of mental capacity is on those who claim that the capacity does not exist.

The living will should clearly state the nature of the treatment and circumstances in which it is to be acted upon and that the nature of the treatment, the circumstances in which it is to be acted upon and the likely effect of the treatment are fully understood by the person making it.

Although there is no Common Law requirement that a living will must be made in writing, in practice it will usually be impossible to give satisfactory proof of the terms of the will and its existence unless it is in writing. It is advisable that any advance directive should be in writing, dated and signed and witnessed by at least one independent witness who will have nothing to gain from the death. The Act will provide that an advance decision must be made in accordance with the formalities set out in the Act if it is to be an effective refusal of 'life-sustaining treatment'.

Life-sustaining treatment is defined by the Act as 'treatment that in the view of the person providing health care for the person concerned is necessary to sustain life'.

When the Act comes into force it will only cover refusal of treatment and will provide that a person over the age of 18, with the requisite mental capacity, will be able to make what in the wording of the Act is called 'an advance decision' to refuse life-sustaining treatment: but only if the refusal is:

◆ made in a document which is signed by the maker, or someone on his behalf and at his direction;

◆ witnessed in his presence; and

◆ states that it is to apply to a treatment even when life is at risk.

There will be a rebuttable presumption that a person has mental capacity, but he has to be able to understand and retain the information relevant to the decision, to use or weigh up the information as part of the process of making the decision and to communicate the decision. If he is unable to fulfil these criteria the person will be considered not to have the requisite mental capacity.

When the Act is in force it will be possible to make a lasting power of attorney to appoint a proxy to make health-care decisions on one's behalf in the event of future incapacity, something which is not possible at the present time.

The Act provides that no life assurance policy shall be invalidated by a physician having assisted a qualifying person to die in accordance with the Act.

Presumably when the Act is passed and comes into force it will be in addition to the Common Law on the subject, in so far as it does not revoke the existing Common Law.

Although a mentally competent adult can refuse a medical treatment by making a living will, he has no legal right to demand a particular treatment; this is in accordance with the doctor's obligation to do what he considers is in the best interest of his patient and his clinical needs. A patient's wish for a particular treatment as expressed in a living will is to be taken into account by the doctor but it is not conclusive and, ultimately, the clinical decision as to what treatment is in the best interest of the patient is to be made by the doctor and not by the patient. Although the doctor makes the decision as to what is in the patient's best interest, he must do so looking at the matter from the particular patient's point of view.

A living will must not have been revoked, even orally or by implication (for example by a change in circumstances), by the time the question of carrying out the treatment arises and, if tested in a court, the court will take into account, but not necessarily follow, the patient's orally expressed wishes, even if the patient is under the age of 18.

If a living will is made it should be frequently reviewed because one's wishes may change in the light of advances in medical science, and unless the maker knows the changes it cannot be said that he is fully aware of the relevant circumstances, treatment and their implications. Care should be taken to ensure that the will and any changes to it are known to the medical practitioner, e.g. by lodging it with him. Discussing the will with the family members could lead to suggestions of undue influence having been applied by them.

A specimen form of living will is included in Appendix 1.

CAPACITY TO DECIDE

Interesting legal questions arise when one does not make an uninfluenced, informed decision to refuse or request treatment to shorten or extend the natural length of one's life or, when one is adjudged not to have sufficient mental capacity to make such a decision. Similar problems arise when, having such capacity and having made the decision, one lacks the physical ability to carry the decision out.

As stated above, a doctor who has in his care a terminally ill but mentally competent patient, whom the doctor treats without the patient's consent, commits a civil and a criminal assault upon the patient, but what constitutes treatment and what is the position if the patient is not in a position to make a proper decision and has not previously given a proper advance directive which remains unchanged on the subject?

Treatment must be distinguished from a withdrawal of basic care such as washing and feeding by spoon as opposed to artificial feeding. Withdrawal of basic care is not permitted; withdrawal of treatment is sometimes permitted.

ACTION IN THE PATIENT'S BEST INTEREST

In a case in which there is no proper consent or refusal and the patient is incapable of giving any, the doctor must do what he considers to be in the best interest of the patient in accordance with a responsible and competent body of relevant professional opinion. This can include innovative treatment not previously tried on human beings if there is evidence from responsible medical opinion that does not reject the treatment. He must ask what can be done for the patient and will it improve the patient's lot? There is a very strong legal presumption that it is in the patient's best interest to preserve his life, but in this context the law does not consider that the prolongation of life is sacrosanct. Other factors such as the patient's assumed wishes, his dignity, mental, physical and spiritual welfare and how tolerable the prolongation of the life is, and will be, are all factors to be weighed in the balance. These factors are only examples and not exclusive. Moreover, the doctor must look at the matter from the point of view of the particular patient.

In the case of an adult patient it is for the doctor to make an informed decision in the light of general medical opinion as to what the patient's best interest is, although in cases of any doubt he should seek advice from a court. If the patient is a child or a ward of court it is for the court to decide, but the child's views and the parents' views will usually be taken into consideration. In neither case is it for a carer or member of the family to decide what is in the patient's best interest.

For a doctor to switch off a life-support machine or withhold artificial feeding or other treatment from an insensate terminally ill patient who has left no valid instructions is not a criminal or civil offence if the doctor considers it is in the patient's best interest. This is because in withdrawing the treatment the doctor is fulfilling his duty to act in the patient's best interest and not introducing an external element, but rather ceasing to treat (omission not commission) and allowing the patient to die of the pre-existing condition. It is not the withdrawal of the support system but the pre-existing condition which kills. A doctor who uses drugs to reduce a terminally ill patient's suffering in the belief that to do so is in the patient's best interest and incidentally hastens the moment of death is legally justified in doing so, but administering a drug with the primary purpose of ending a patient's life is unlawful, whether or not it is the patient's wish.

IS THERE A RIGHT TO DIE?

Withdrawal of or failure to supply medical treatment with the patient's proper consent or at the patient's request is not to be confused with the patient having a right to die, even if death will inevitably follow. The European Court has confirmed in the case of *Pretty* v *The United Kingdom* that there is no general right to die as such in English law. If the patient is mentally competent but physically incapable, a general right to die would involve the assistance of others in the withdrawal of basic care or the introduction of a positive element with the primary intention of causing death, both of which are unlawful euthanasia. Even the Assisted Dying for the

Terminally Ill Bill, presently under consideration by Parliament, only contemplates the provision of the means for the patient to take his own life and not the active taking of life by another. Hence if the patient is physically incapable of taking his own life the bill will not assist.

INTENTIONALLY AND ACCIDENTALLY CAUSING DEATH

For a doctor to withdraw or fail to supply medical treatment with the patient's proper consent or at the patient's request is not the same thing as for a third party to surreptitiously disconnect a life-support system: the doctor is allowing the patient to die from the pre-existing condition, but the third party is preventing the doctor from prolonging the patient's life.

To cause another's death intentionally and without lawful justification constitutes murder, or if the death is caused without intention but with gross negligence, manslaughter, and in either case there is a civil assault giving a right to damages which survives the death.

If the death of another is caused unintentionally and without negligence it is accidental death, for which there is no civil or criminal liability, unless the act which caused the death was in breach of a duty imposed upon the perpetrator by statute, in which case there are both criminal and civil liabilities. To cause the death of another by an act which is not gross negligence, but which could be foreseen to cause harm but not necessarily death, is a civil offence which gives rise to a claim for damages.

FAILURE TO ASSIST

A failure to assist another which results in death does not incur a liability for damages or criminal liability, unless the person who fails to act has undertaken a duty of care to the person who dies, e.g. as in the doctor and patient relationship. The question of whether Article 2 of the European Convention on Human Rights (The Right to Life) is breached by the failure of English law to impose a duty upon individuals to assist is questionable.

LEGAL CONSEQUENCES OF PROLONGING LIFE

Although they cannot legally be taken into account when deciding whether or not to do so, the ability to artificially prolong life may have legal consequences other than the criminal. For example, it can alter rights of inheritance in a particular case, it may alter pension entitlements or the amount of income or inheritance tax payable if life is prolonged into a new tax year in which rates or allowances are changed, and it can affect the size of the damages in road traffic accident cases.

Steps to Take and the Procedures following Death

URGENT PRACTICAL MATTERS

The following things need to be done by the executor or next of kin as soon as possible after a death has taken place:

- obtain medical certification of the death from the doctor or from the midwife in the case of a stillbirth;

- register the death with the Registrar of Births, Deaths and Marriages;

- search for any will and possible later wills (remember to check under alternative names e.g. nicknames and aliases);

- search for documents indicating the deceased's wishes in relation to the funeral;

- arrange and carry out the funeral;

- notify anyone to whom the deceased had given a power of attorney and any Receiver appointed by The Court of Protection of the death (their powers cease at the time of the death);

- remove portable valuables to a secure location and ensure that they have adequate insurance cover at that location;

- search for household goods, motor vehicle and building insurance policies; check that cover exists and is appropriate and adequate and if not amend it. Notify the insurers of the removal of any items which have been removed from the deceased's home for safe custody and amend the cover into the executor's or proposed administrator's names. If policies cannot be found, effect new policies in the executor's or proposed administrator's names;

- arrange with the postal authority to redirect the deceased's mail and contact The Mail Preference Service to stop unwanted junk mail;

- notify anyone from whom the deceased received an annuity or pension and the Pensions Service of the death and claim any new benefits which arise by virtue of the death;

- inform the deceased's bank and any debit or credit card providers of the death;

- inform the trustees of any trust from which the deceased received a benefit of the death;

- notify the tenant of any property which the deceased owned and let of the death and request payments of future rents be made to the executors or proposed administrators of the estate;

- notify the registrars of all known shareholdings, and stock exchange or other investments of the death;

- inform all known creditors (including any mortgage company) of the death and request confirmation of the amount of the debt and forbearance until the estate is in funds;

◆ notify the supply companies for domestic services of the death and request continuance or termination of service as required; if relevant request new meter readings be made and redirection of accounts; and

◆ in relation to council tax, notify the local authority of the death and if appropriate claim a single occupancy discount.

If required, more detailed information on these practical matters can be found in the index and examples of the letters to use can be found in the appendix.

SUMMARY OF PROCEDURES

When a death has taken place the doctor issues a certificate confirming death and its cause. If the cause of death is not clear or not from natural causes, the doctor will report the death to the coroner who will order a post mortem examination to take place. After the post mortem examination, if it is still not clear that the death is from natural causes, an inquest will be held. When the doctor has issued a death certificate the death must be registered with the Registrar of Births, Deaths and Marriages who will issue his death certificate and a certificate for burial, or cremation, which must be taken to the funeral director before the funeral can take place. If an inquest has been held the certificate for burial or cremation can be collected from the coroner's office who will then send the particulars required to register the death directly to the Registrar of Births Deaths and Marriages. There is no necessity for anyone to attend the resulting registration. These matters are discussed in greater detail in the following pages.

THE DOCTOR'S CERTIFICATE

If the death takes place in hospital or in a nursing home, the hospital or home will arrange the issue of a doctor's medical certificate confirming death and its cause.

The certificate is given in a sealed envelope and must be issued before the funeral can be arranged or the death registered with the Registrar of Births Deaths and Marriages. The doctor will also give another certificate which is a formal notice explaining the procedure to register the death and confirming that the medical certificate has been given. The medical certificate must be taken to the Registrar unopened within five days of being issued or within forty-two days in the case of a stillbirth. A stillbirth is the birth of a baby who is born dead after the 24th week of pregnancy. If the birth is a stillbirth the doctor or sometimes the midwife will give a Certificate of Stillbirth instead of the certificate confirming the cause of death. A stillborn baby can be named and the stillbirth must be registered and can sometimes be registered at the hospital instead of at the Registrar's but it cannot be registered after three months. A certificate for burial or cremation of a stillborn baby must be obtained from the registrar before its funeral can take place.

When death occurs at home, the patient's own doctor should be called. He will issue the certificates unless he has not seen the person who has died and who is called the deceased within the previous 14 days, in which case he will have to report the death to the coroner.

CORONERS

The Department of Constitutional Affairs is responsible for matters relating to coroners, but coroners are officials who are independent of the national government, the local authority and the police. The coroner is a lawyer or a doctor and sometimes both!

In the following additional cases the death will be reported to the coroner:

◆ accidental death;

◆ sudden unexpected death;

◆ where the cause of death is uncertain;

◆ if the death is thought to be the result of industrial disease;

◆ violent death;

◆ when death occurred in suspicious circumstances;

◆ death in the custody of the police or prison authorities;

◆ death during the course of an operation or before recovery from the anaesthetic.

Anyone can report a death to the coroner through the coroner's officer whose contact details can be obtained from the local police.

The coroner's power to enquire into deaths within his jurisdiction also applies to deaths abroad, at sea or in the air, if the body is brought into the coroner's area, for example by a ship bringing the body into a harbour within his area.

Under sections 271–273 of the Merchant Shipping Act 1995, in cases where:

◆ death occurs on a British ship; or

◆ the master of a British ship dies outside the United Kingdom; or

◆ the death of a seaman occurs outside the United Kingdom as a result of injury or disease suffered while or within one year of serving on a British ship; then

unless a coroner's inquest is to be held, an enquiry must be held by the superintendent or proper officer of the next port at which the ship calls and a copy of the report of the enquiry will be given, upon request, to the next of kin or any person whom the Secretary of State considers to have a valid interest in it. This provision can prove useful in appropriate circumstances if a claim for compensation is contemplated.

In the case of deaths:

◆ in or from United Kingdom ships;

◆ of Citizens of the UK and its Colonies in or from ships which come into British ports; or

◆ abroad of seamen employed in UK registered ships,

the Registrar General of Shipping and Seamen will issue death certificates and the deaths are recorded at the Registry of Shipping and Seamen at Anchor House, 12 Cheviot Close, Parc – Ty-Glas, Llanishen, Cardiff CF14 5JA, Telephone 02920 768200. The deaths are also recorded at the General Registry Office in London, Belfast, Edinburgh and the Isle of Man as appropriate in the Marine Register of Deaths.

Deaths and presumed deaths on or from offshore installations are also registered with the Registrar of Shipping and Seamen and copies registered with The Registrar General of Births and Deaths.

If a death is reported to the coroner, certificates to enable the death to be registered and to authorise a funeral to take place will be issued by the coroner and not by the doctor, but not until a post mortem examination of the body and possibly an inquest has taken place. This applies whether or not the death takes place at home, in a nursing home or in a hospital.

A post mortem is an examination of the body by a pathologist. Relatives have the right to choose a doctor to represent them at the post mortem, but no right to object to the holding of a post mortem ordered by a coroner which should not be confused with a post mortem requested by a hospital. A post mortem requested by a hospital cannot be carried out without the consent of the next of kin or executors of the deceased's will.

INQUESTS
In the following cases the coroner will hold an inquest:

- if after the post mortem examination the cause of death remains uncertain;

- if the death appears to have been an unnatural or a violent one;

- where the death occurred in prison;

- when the death appears to have been caused by a reportable industrial disease.

If anyone is charged with an offence that constitutes homicide in one form or another, the inquest will be adjourned.

The coroner holds the inquest in public and its sole purpose is to ascertain:

◆ who the deceased was;

◆ the particulars required to be registered by the registrar concerning the death; and

◆ how, when, where and by what means the deceased came to die.

'How' means in what circumstances and the inquest can comment not only upon the immediate cause of death but also upon the facts surrounding the death and can make recommendations as to how similar deaths can be avoided in the future. The verdict, i.e. conclusion of the inquest, must express an opinion on any disputed facts and acts; omissions can be recorded, but not in such a way as to amount to a finding of criminal liability in respect of a named person nor to determine civil liability. Expressions such as 'carelessness', 'neglect', and 'negligence' must not be used. The purpose of an inquest is not to apportion blame and the coroner's verdict does not preclude further proceedings in the civil or criminal courts.

Coroners' verdicts are decided on a balance of probability unless the verdict is one of unlawful killing or suicide, both of which must be proved beyond reasonable doubt. If the evidence is not sufficient to come to a specific conclusion an open verdict will be entered.

There is no appeal as such from the verdict of an inquest but if new evidence comes to light, or it is believed that an error of law has been made, it is possible to seek a judicial review by the High Court or to ask the Attorney General for permission to refer the case to the High Court.

In holding an inquest a coroner is conducting a hearing in a court of law and, although proceedings are kept fairly informal and are determined to a large extent by the individual coroner, he has the power to compel witnesses to attend and takes evidence on oath. Anyone who wishes to give evidence at an inquest or question a witness should inform the coroner in advance so that the inquest can proceed in an orderly manner. Sometimes the coroner will have a jury to assist him in coming to his verdict, which is technically known as a 'conclusion'. The jury consists of between seven and eleven people selected at random as for other juries and can bring in a majority verdict. There is a legal right for relatives of the deceased, and anyone with a proper interest in the outcome of the proceedings, to attend the inquest if they wish and to ask questions relevant to the circumstances and cause of death. There is no right for anyone to make speeches. Relatives of the deceased also have the right to be represented by a lawyer, but legal aid is not usually granted for the purpose of representation at inquests. There is a charity called Inquest Charitable Trust ('Inquest'), which provides free advice to bereaved families on their rights and procedures in Coroners' Courts; sometimes it is able to arrange for families to be legally represented in Coroners' Courts free of charge or at a reduced charge. (Contact details can be found in the Useful Addresses section of the appendix.) It is wise to be legally represented at an inquest if claims by the deceased's estate for compensation arising from the circumstances of the death are likely, and if requested a coroner might supply a copy of notes of the evidence given at the inquest.

A coroner's inquest is sufficient to fulfil the duty imposed upon the State by Article 2 of the European Convention on Human Rights to set up a legal framework to protect life, and to ensure that if a death occurs in custody there is a reasonably prompt and effective investigation before an independent body with an opportunity for the deceased's relatives to take part. Deaths in custody are also investigated by The Prisons and Probation Ombudsman.

At the conclusion of the inquest the coroner will issue a Certificate after Inquest (form 99 (rev)) which states the cause of death. This is then sent to the Registrar of Births, Deaths and Marriages so that registration of the death can take place where either a Certificate for Cremation (Form E) or an Order for Burial (form 101), is issued so that the funeral can take place. If the inquest is likely to be a lengthy one, the coroner can issue Form 101 or Form E before the conclusion of the inquest if he is satisfied that the body is no longer required.

ORGAN TRANSPLANTS AND MEDICAL RESEARCH

If the death is one which should be reported to a coroner, the coroner's consent will be required before the body can be used for organ transplants or other medical purposes.

If the body is to be used for medical research, ask the medical attendant to make the necessary arrangements or contact the Inspector of Anatomy at the Anatomy Office of the nearest teaching hospital. In case of difficulty telephone HM Inspector of Anatomy on 020 7972 4342. A hospital is not obliged to accept a body for teaching purposes and it will not be accepted if unsuitable, for example if a post mortem has taken place. If accepted for teaching purposes, the body might be kept for up to three years.

A person lawfully in possession of a body can give consent to an organ transplant if, after the making of reasonable enquiries, he has no reason to believe that the deceased or his close relatives would object, or if the deceased had either made and not withdrawn an oral consent in the presence of two witnesses or a written consent. Common ways of showing consent to organs being used for transplant purposes are:

◆ carrying a signed donor card obtainable from most doctors' surgeries and hospitals;

◆ requesting a note of consent to be made on a driving licence when it is applied for;

◆ requesting that an entry be made by the NHS Organ Registration Service upon the organ donors' register. This can be done by post and the address can be found in the Useful Addresses section of the appendix or online at www.uktransplant.org.uk;

◆ including the request in a will.

If it is intended that parts of the body shall be used for an organ transplant, it is essential that the medical attendant be informed as soon as possible because the organs will be of no value if they are not removed promptly.

If tissue from the body is to be donated for research it must similarly be removed promptly. A tissue bank is maintained by the Histology Department of the Peterborough District Hospital which will collect and return bodies within a 150-mile radius. They are usually kept for about 24 hours and the tissue is used for research into pharmaceutical products.

This might appeal to those who object to the testing of drugs on animals.

REGISTERING THE DEATH

When the doctor's certificate as to the cause of death has been obtained, it is necessary to register the death with a Registrar of Births, Deaths and Marriages within five days, or in the case of a stillbirth, within 42 days. The particulars for registration may be given to any registrar who will forward them to the registrar for the subdistrict in which the death took place, where it will be officially registered.

The addresses of the registrars can be obtained from the local telephone book, local council, the doctor, hospital or nursing home.

Some registrars require an appointment to be made to save waiting, so it is a good idea to telephone first.

WHO CAN REGISTER A DEATH?

The following people can register a death:

◆ a relative;

◆ a person present at the death;

◆ the owner or manager of the nursing home where the death took place;

◆ the person causing the body to be disposed of; or

◆ a person who has custody of the body.

If an inquest has taken place the coroner will arrange the registration of the death.

THE PARTICULARS REQUIRED

The information which is required to be given is the full names and addresses of the person registering the death and of the person who has died (including the maiden name of the deceased in the case of a woman), the date and place of birth of the deceased, his occupation and last usual address, the date of the death and the location where it took place, and particulars of any allowance or pension which the deceased was receiving from public funds. If the deceased was married or had a registered civil partner, the person registering the death will also be required to state the full name, occupation and date of birth of the surviving spouse or civil partner. The doctor's certificate as to the cause of death, or in the case of a stillbirth the Medical Certificate of Stillbirth, will have to be handed to the registrar, so remember to take along all the information, the deceased's medical card and the certificates.

HOW THE DEATH IS REGISTERED

From the information supplied the registrar prepares draft entries for the Register of Deaths which the person attending to register the death is asked to check. The registrar then enters the information in the register and the informant is asked to check and sign the register entries using the registrar's pen which contains indelible ink. The informant should check the register carefully before the Registrar signs it because once the registrar has signed the entries cannot be corrected without supporting documentary evidence, and in some cases without the consent of the Registrar General.

If the particulars are given to the registrar for the subdistrict in which the death took place, the registrar will give to the person supplying the information a registrar's death certificate, or in the case of a stillbirth a Certificate of Registration of Stillbirth, and ask if any official copies of the certificate are required. There is a fee for the death certificate and for each copy, but it is cheaper if copies are obtained when registering the death than if they are obtained later. Some copies will be needed to avoid delay later. I suggest that a copy for each relative who has the deceased's life insured and three copies in addition to the original of the registrar's copy is a sensible practical number. The fee is currently £3.50 for each copy if acquired when registering the death and £7.00 for each copy acquired later, but when the register of deaths has been passed to The General Register Office in London, the fee is £8.50 with a further £3.00 fee if the original certificate reference is not known and a search has to be made. The certificates can be ordered by post, telephone or fax and if ordered online the fee is £7.00. A priority next day service is now available at a fee of £27.50 or £23.00 if the applicant supplies the certificate reference.

Copyright law covers registrars' certificates and photocopying without licence is not permissible.

The Registrar will also supply a free certificate of registration of death (form BD8), usable only for Social Security purposes.

Unless the coroner has been involved and issued one, the registrar will also give a certificate (known as the Green Form) authorising the funeral to take place. If an inquest is lengthy it is sometimes possible to obtain an Order for Burial (form 101) or a certificate for cremation (form E) from the coroner before the conclusion of the inquest, if he is satisfied that the body is no longer required.

Provided that he has the doctor's certificate as to the cause of death, the registrar can give the Green Form before registration has been completed and it will be valid as the authority for burial, but only Green Forms given *after* registration are valid for cremation.

If the particulars are given to the registrar of a subdistrict other than the one in which the death took place, the certificates will be sent by post.

DEATHS ABROAD

Although there is no statutory requirement to register the death in England or Wales if the death takes place on a foreign registered ship or aircraft or abroad (which for this purpose includes in Scotland, Northern and Southern Ireland) the death should be registered (a) with the British Consulate and (b) in accordance with the law and procedures of the country concerned.

Registration of the death with the British Consulate enables one to obtain copies of the death certificate from the consulate or from the Overseas Registration Section, Smedleys Hydro, Trafalgar Road, Birkdale, Southport PR8 2HH.

If the death takes place out of the United Kingdom the British Consulate will be prepared to help with advice on the formalities for registering the death abroad and the procedures involved in returning the body to the United Kingdom.

(3)

Arranging the Funeral

Who arranges the funeral? If there is a will the executors are entitled to claim the body and have the right and duty to dispose of it and arrange the funeral. If there is no will the person primarily entitled to obtain a grant of letters of administration of the estate on intestacy is the person entitled to these rights. (See chapter 7 pages 66 and 67 as to who that person is.)

What happens if there are several people equally entitled who wish to deal with it differently? An Australian case suggests that because of the need to deal with the matter quickly, if one person has already made proper arrangements, for practical reasons that person's wishes will be preferred.

Remember that the person who arranges the funeral is contractually responsible for paying for it.

If death takes place in hospital and there is nobody who is prepared to arrange and pay for the funeral, the Local Health Authority can arrange a basic funeral and can claim the cost from the deceased's estate. As a last resort if the body is not claimed the local authority will arrange a basic funeral at the expense of the estate. In any case where the local authority arranges the funeral it is not permitted to cause the body to be cremated if it has reason to believe that to do so would be contrary to the deceased's wishes. If the funeral is for a stillborn child (whether born at home or in hospital), the local hospital will usually be prepared to provide a free funeral. Maternity benefits may also be payable in cases of a stillbirth as well as in the case of a live birth. Although it is the executor's duty and right to arrange the funeral, in practice the family usually arranges the funeral.

The funeral can take place as soon as is desired after the issue of the certificate for burial or cremation, or it can be delayed for a reasonable period to suit the family, but before the funeral can take place, apart from registering the death, there are other matters to be dealt with and decisions to be made.

The body will have to be 'laid out', that is washed and the eyes and mouth closed and the limbs straightened before 'rigor mortis' (stiffening of the of the limbs) takes place. The deceased will be dressed in his funeral clothes which can be his own clothes or a gown, called a shroud, provided by the funeral director. These services can, but need not necessarily, be provided by the hospital if death takes place in hospital or by the funeral director. Usually the deceased will be taken from the place of death to the undertaker's chapel of rest where he will be kept in cool conditions to await the funeral.

The body may be given 'hygienic treatment', sometimes referred to as 'embalming', to preserve its appearance and delay decomposition. Hygienic treatment consists of substitution of a solution of formalin for the blood. Tell the funeral director whether or not this is required. Usually a 'Green' or woodland burial of embalmed bodies is not permitted.

If the family and friends wish they can visit the deceased in the chapel of rest by arrangement with the funeral director.

It will be necessary to decide where the funeral shall take place, whether the body is to be buried or cremated and if cremated what is to happen to the ashes.

The deceased may have left instructions in or with a will or spoken with family or friends as regards a preference for burial or cremation and as regards the form of the funeral. Whilst the decision of any executor with regard to these matters and place where the funeral shall take place is final (unless the law itself has required burial instead of cremation), it is usual to honour the deceased's wishes. The law will not forbid cremation unless there has been a suspicion of foul play.

Although directions in a will concerning the funeral and disposal of a body are not binding, the deceased can perhaps achieve his wishes by leaving a legacy to his executor which is made conditional upon them being carried out!

If it is intended to take a body out of England and Wales (for example for a funeral), the coroner's permission must be obtained at least four days before removal takes place, whether or not it has been necessary to report the death to the coroner.

BRINGING A BODY BACK FROM ABROAD

The body of a person who has died on a foreign ship or aircraft or out of England or Wales ('abroad') can be brought back to England or Wales for a funeral, but it is expensive to do so and a death certificate and authority to return the body will have to be obtained from the relevant foreign country. It will be cheaper to cremate the body abroad and return the ashes but not all foreign countries have facilities for cremation.

The circumstances in which it is necessary to report a death to the coroner in the case of a death within his area in England

and Wales also make it necessary to report the death to the coroner if the body is brought within his area from abroad.

Before the funeral of a person who died abroad can be arranged in England or Wales it is necessary to obtain a Certificate of No Liability to Register the death from the registrar of the subdistrict in which it is proposed that the funeral shall take place, unless a coroner's authority for burial or cremation has been obtained, or the death has been registered with the British consul. It is advisable to register the death with the British consul in addition to registration with the foreign authorities, so that there will be a record in Britain of the death and it will be possible to obtain a copy death certificate from The Nationality and Passport Section of the Foreign and Commonwealth Office, which is only open on weekday mornings. If the funeral is to be a cremation, either authority from the Coroners Section of the Home Office or (if the death is not the result of natural causes) a certificate for cremation from the coroner is also required. Additionally it is necessary to produce an authenticated translation of the foreign death certificate which shows the cause of death.

HIV/AIDS

Although AIDS and HIV are not diseases which are notifiable under the Public Health Act 1984, the Public Health (Infectious Diseases) Regulations 1998 (SI 1998 No. 1546) applies sections 43 and 44 of the Act to AIDS and HIV.

Section 43 authorises a local authority or doctor to prevent the removal of the body of a person who has died from AIDS from hospital except direct to a mortuary or for burial or cremation and Section 44 imposes a duty upon a person in whose house a person has died from AIDS to take reasonably practical steps to prevent anyone coming into contact with the body unnecessarily. Breaches of these provisions are backed by criminal sanctions but in practice they are seldom enforced.

In cases of death following HIV or AIDS advice can be obtained from FACTS Health Centre, the Terrence Higgins Trust or the London Lighthouse Trust.

BURIAL OR CREMATION?

Cremation is considerably cheaper than burial and far more cremations take place in Britain than burials. The shortage of land for burials is acute, but many people have deep emotional, intellectual and religious feelings and beliefs as to whether they should be buried or cremated. Muslims and Orthodox Jews require burial, Buddhists and Hindus cremation. Sikhs will only permit cremation and request that their ashes be scattered in a river or sea. Non-Orthodox Jews will sometimes permit cremation. Some Christians request cremation, some burial.

If a young child is cremated there will probably be no ashes to be disposed of and consequently little in the sense of a place of memorial to visit. Any pacemaker must be removed before cremation to prevent a possible explosion, and if a crematorium medical referee is not satisfied with the additional medical forms which have to be completed for a cremation he can order a post mortem which cannot be refused, so if interference with the body after death disturbs you or you find it distasteful, choose burial. On the other hand a grave in a churchyard or municipal cemetery cannot be purchased; it is only leased for a number of years after which it might be re-used. Unless exclusive burial rights are purchased the grave is known as a 'common grave' and even after a few years strangers may be buried in it and sole occupancy lost.

Those churchyards that are not already full and closed to burials are filling up very quickly and there is a common law right for all who:

- live or die in a parish; or

- are on the parish electoral roll

to be buried in the churchyard unless it has been closed by due process of law. Further, as one judge put it, 'It cannot be said that the churchyard is nearly full by considering only the areas which have never been used for burials. No churchyard is full and ripe for closure until all the parts of it in which reburial is possible have been buried over again at least once and until closure all burial rights continue.' Reuse of graves is encouraged if the previous burial took place at least 75 years ago and there is no relative who is likely to be distressed by the removal of the headstone. Closed burial grounds are sometimes built over.

Although one might have a right to be buried in a churchyard there is no right to be buried in a particular place in the churchyard. That is a matter to be decided by the incumbent minister unless a faculty (i.e. an order from the church court for the diocese) reserving a right of burial in a specified grave space has been granted. It is possible to reserve a right of burial in a churchyard by petitioning and obtaining a faculty if one is entitled to be buried there; the fact that such a reservation will prejudice the rights of parishioners who may wish to be buried there in the future is not a ground for refusal of the petition. Anyone who is presently entitled to be buried in a particular churchyard and has a strong desire to do so because family members are buried there, or because they have strong connections with the parish but might move out of the parish, should consider applying for a faculty now, especially if space in the churchyard is scarce.

Subject to general guidance from the parochial church council, the incumbent as the freeholder of the churchyard may authorise the burial there of the remains of a person who would otherwise have no right of burial in the churchyard and no faculty will be granted for the burial of any such remains without the consent of the incumbent.

For a cremation, unless a coroner has issued a certificate for cremation, two cremation certificates signed by different doctors and a certificate for cremation issued by the Registrar are required, but if a funeral director is employed he will arrange for and deal with them.

Although a cremation can only take place at an authorised crematorium ashes can be buried on one's own private land, on the land of another with the owner's permission or scattered at sea and they can be disposed of with or without family and friends being present. After burial they cannot be removed later without permission from the Home Office.

Cremated remains may be buried in the Garden of Remembrance of the crematorium where cremation takes place or of another crematorium. Many crematoria no longer permit the scattering of ashes in the Remembrance Garden or the burial of containers; the ashes are buried directly into the soil.

Some churchyards and cemeteries have areas for burial of cremated remains and may permit them to be buried in a container even if they are full for burial of uncremated bodies. Burial of the ashes in a family grave which is considered to be full for the purpose of non-cremated remains is sometimes permitted.

If cremated ashes are to be taken abroad some countries require the container containing the ashes to be sealed in the presence of embassy staff and Customs and Excise will require a certificate from the crematorium where cremation has take place.

ALTERNATIVE FUNERAL ARRANGEMENTS

A funeral can be arranged and carried out with or without the assistance of a funeral director.

'Green' and 'DIY' burials

Although cremation can only take place at a licensed crematorium there are few regulations governing burial, provided the death has been registered with the Registrar and his certificate for burial or a coroner's order for burial has been issued.

Instead of a traditional funeral carried out by a professional funeral director in a churchyard, municipal cemetery or crematorium, some people prefer a 'green' funeral. Green funerals can be carried out by the family with or without the assistance of a funeral director and burials can take place on private land with the owner's permission. Instead of the usual hardwood or veneered chipboard coffin, a cheaper and more environmentally friendly biodegradable cardboard or wicker coffin may be used, but for a cremation the coffin must comply with the crematorium's specifications. Environmentally friendly biodegradable coffins and environmentally friendly accessories can be obtained from Vic Fearn Ltd. or Compakta Ltd whose contact details are set out in the useful addresses section of the appendix. The website www.uk-funerals.co.uk

contains information and lists of suppliers, funeral directors and monumental masons which will prove useful when arranging a funeral without a professional funeral director. Advice on arranging a 'green', 'woodland' or 'DIY' funeral can also be obtained from The Natural Death Centre, a non-profit-making charity which publishes information and is prepared to e-mail information and advice on the subject. Its principal publication, 'The New Natural Death Handbook', is a source of information as to such matters as available woodland burial sites and suppliers of funeral goods such as urns, shrouds, and cardboard or traditional coffins by overnight mail order.

Anyone considering a 'DIY' funeral must give some thought to collection and storage of the body pending burial, removal of any pacemaker if the body is to be cremated and to safety considerations when digging the grave. The body should be covered by at least 0.91 metres of soil. A body can begin to deteriorate soon after death and it needs to be kept cool and pacemakers must be removed before cremation to prevent a possible explosion. Some but not all professional funeral directors are prepared to assist with these matters without carrying out the remainder of the funeral.

Although burial does not have to take place in a churchyard or cemetery, it must not constitute a danger to public health or pose a pollution threat to the water supply, and it is as well to check first and in good time that the local authority has no objection. A check should also be made to ensure that the digging of the grave will not interfere with gas, electricity and other services. If it is proposed to carry out the burial in the garden of the deceased's home careful thought should be given to the resale value of the property and the problem of tending the grave if the property is sold at a future date. To bury a body on another person's land without their permission would be illegal as constituting a trespass to the land. Whenever a burial takes place on private land, it is wise to check the title deeds to ensure that they do not contain restrictions on the use of the land which prevent the use of the land for burial purposes. It is also wise to keep a record of the site of the burial with the title deeds because it is illegal to disturb a grave without permission from the Home Office. The Registrar of Deaths must be notified of the date and place within 96 hours of the burial, and the full name and age of the deceased, and date of death noted on the coffin lid.

A burial must not disturb a recognised archaeological site and any grave marker, high fencing or wall or multiple burials might require planning permission.

Burial at sea
Burial at sea is better arranged with the assistance of a professional funeral director. A licence from the Department of the Environment, Farming and Rural Affairs and a special coffin are required. It can only take place in certain parts of the sea off Newhaven and the Isle of Wight and the coroner's permission is required to take the body out of the country. Such burials are expensive.

FUNERALS WITH THE AID OF A PROFESSIONAL FUNERAL DIRECTOR
To arrange a funeral with the assistance of a professional funeral director, take the registrar's copy of the death certificate and either the registrar's or the coroner's certificate for burial or cremation to the funeral director. If the deceased died abroad, also take a Scottish or Irish death certificate or an authenticated translation of the foreign death certificate (as appropriate) and the Certificate of No Liability to Register or

Coroner's certificate for cremation or burial. Agree the arrangements (place, time, burial or cremation, type of coffin, number of cars, minister to officiate at the ceremony, etc.) with the undertaker. Check that the proposed burial ground is not likely to object to the type of headstone or other memorial that you have in mind, because churches and municipal cemetery proprietors are becoming increasingly particular as to what they will allow.

There is no legal requirement for funeral directors to be licensed or have training or any form of qualification, but most belong to a recognised professional body with a code of practice. Unless you have previous experience of the funeral director or he has been recommended to you it is as well to check these matters out before instructing him.

The role of a funeral director is that of adviser, organiser and supplier of services. A good funeral director will give you expert advice and practical help, accept responsibility for making most of the arrangements and he will fit in with your personal needs, wishes and ethnic customs. He will be understanding and provide emotional support. Most funeral directors have a chapel of rest where the body can be temporarily kept and visited. They can advise upon choice of coffin (wooden, cardboard, wicker basket type or metal container). If required some will arrange catering facilities, house sitting, the use of horse drawn vehicles and the photography and video services for which some people feel a need. The undertaker can also arrange publication of any obituary notices that might be desired, any donations to a favourite charity and floral tributes, or you can arrange these yourself or dispense with them.

When instructing a funeral director obtain a quotation for the cost of the funeral and check what services are offered and exactly what is included in the fee. Most directors will offer a package including the collection of the body, hygienic treatment (sometimes called embalming or cosmetic treatment) of the body, a choice of coffins, use of a chapel of rest, the making of arrangements with and completion of the necessary documentation for the cemetery or crematorium, the engagement of any required minister of religion and music, newspaper obituaries, transportation and payment of the fees for the cemetery or crematorium, the minister and other expenses. If some items in the package are not required it might be possible to negotiate a lower charge.

Floral tributes may be sent direct to the funeral director or to the place where the principal mourners will meet on the day of the funeral. If cremation has been decided upon, at many crematoria the floral tributes will be disposed of after a few hours and one might prefer to give instructions that cut flowers go to a local hospital instead. If so requested the funeral director will arrange to collect any cards sent with the floral tributes and pass them to the family after the funeral has taken place.

In the case of cremation it will usually be necessary to decide what is to be done with the ashes, but in the case of babies there may be no ashes.

If there is to be a religious ceremony but neither those who arrange the funeral nor the deceased have any contact with a minister, the funeral director can arrange for a minister to conduct the ceremony. If a non-religious ceremony is required the British Humanist Society can assist in making contact with someone to officiate. The person who is to conduct the ceremony will arrange a meeting to obtain information for his eulogy about the person who has died and to discuss anything required by the family or the deceased as to the form of the service, e.g. music, readings, any lying in church or requiem mass, etc. Friends and relatives may be invited to speak at the ceremony and should be notified of the date, time and place of the funeral. One should try to ascertain how many will attend the funeral and require transport to the church and how many will stay for refreshments after the funeral. It is usual to issue a general invitation to those attending the funeral (or at least to ask the closest friends and relatives attending) to return to the house or to repair to a local restaurant or pub for light refreshments. Some of those attending may have put themselves out or travelled a long way to attend.

MEMORIALS

If it is intended that there shall be any form of memorial such as a plaque or headstone, then before the funeral is arranged, enquiry should be made of those who manage the proposed site as to whether the proposed memorial and inscription is of a type and material that is likely to be permitted. Never order a memorial without checking this and the cost (including the cost of delivery and erection).

Cemeteries and churchyards enforce their regulations strictly.

In the case of St. Peter's Limpsfield, which was decided by the ecclesiastical court for the diocese of Southwark in June 2004, even though the deceased had been a churchwarden at the church, permission to erect a memorial to him in the churchyard was refused because he was buried elsewhere. It was pointed out that churchyards were primarily for the burial of human remains in consecrated ground and the purpose of permitted memorials was to enable relatives and others to know where the remains were interred. Any other information which might be permitted (for example, information as to the deceased's achievements in life) was considered to be secondary. Memorials to community events, such as war memorials, were permitted as exceptions and other memorials (in the strict sense of the word) would not be permitted because they would utilise scarce space that might otherwise be available for burials.

$$\left(4\right)$$

The Funeral

THE CEREMONY

No ceremony is necessary at a funeral but it is unusual not to
have one. If there is to be a ceremony it need not be a religious
one and can follow any form, but if clergy are to be involved
in a ceremony, they will insist that nothing which is contrary
to their beliefs or senses of decorum and propriety is included.
If there is to be a religious ceremony the coffin is sometimes
taken to the church the previous evening to await the funeral
service, but more usually on the day of the funeral.

On the day of the funeral, if the coffin has not lain in the
church overnight, the hearse and any additional cars arrive at
the place where the principal mourners have met (usually the
deceased's house or a relative's house) before proceeding to
the church, cemetery or crematorium. If there is to be a
ceremony the chief mourners lead the other mourners into the
church or crematorium chapel following the coffin and sit in
the front row. If there is to be a burial after the ceremony
mourners follow the coffin to the grave where a much shorter
ceremony of committal takes place as the coffin is lowered into
the grave. Sometimes the family request that the committal is
a private committal restricted to the family and a few chosen
close friends. After the burial (or after the ceremony if a
cremation and not a burial is involved) the chief mourners
stop for a few minutes to thank the other mourners for
attending and then all are free to leave.

It has been known for burglars to scan the press for details of forthcoming funerals and the deceased's address should not be given in any press notices. Sometimes it is arranged for 'house-sitters' to stay in the house while the funeral takes place for security purposes and to ensure that refreshments are ready and to welcome the mourners when they return.

DEALING WITH COMPLAINTS

If there is a complaint against the funeral director, first make a direct approach to him. If the complaint cannot be resolved directly with him, try contacting the local authority's Trading Standards Department. If it proves impossible to resolve a complaint against a funeral director who is a member of a trade association which has a conciliation scheme, a request to the association to look at the matter under its scheme might bring a satisfactory result. If all else fails one can always seek redress through the local small claims court.

MEETING THE COSTS OF THE FUNERAL

The person who arranges the funeral is contractually liable to pay the bill, but an executor or the administrator of an estate who pays for the funeral has a legal right to be reimbursed by the estate if the deceased's estate is sufficient to cover the cost. If there is no one able or willing to meet the cost of the funeral, the local authority or, if the deceased died in hospital, the local health authority for the area in which the deceased died will arrange the funeral. If the health authority or local authority arrange and pay for the funeral they also have a right to reimbursement from the estate.

Existing grave space

A search through the deceased's papers might produce a deed of grave space showing that space in an existing grave or a new grave has already been paid for, but remember that the cost of the funeral is more than the cost of a grave. A hearse, funeral cars, any minister and grave diggers, etc. all have to be paid for, so it is as well to get a quotation before entering into a commitment.

Funeral prepayment plans

The deceased may have made arrangements for payment of the cost of the funeral to be made from a funeral prepayment plan, and some occupational pension schemes, professional bodies, provident clubs and trade unions might make a payment towards funeral costs.

Many funeral prepayment plans have the advantage that the funeral is paid for at the prices prevalent at the date of payment and the worries of inflation and future financial difficulty are avoided. It is vital that anyone considering taking out a plan for their own funeral must read the small print and check exactly what is included, and whether or not the plan is inflation proof. Although such plans may protect against inflation they have the disadvantage that the cost is paid up front, earns no interest and provides no income for the payer from the time it is paid.

It is also necessary when contemplating a plan to be certain it has a sound financial base and that that there will be adequate funds available if the plan provider is in liquidation or has disappeared at the appropriate time. If a provider is authorised by the Financial Services Authority the plan will be covered by its compensation scheme. If it is not regulated by the FSA, at least check that its funds are held in a trust fund that has a major bank or insurance company as the trustee, that the fund's accounts are regularly audited and are invested upon the advice of a well known and long established FSA licensed investment manager.

Membership of the Cremation Society or private crematoria

Shareholders in certain funeral companies and private crematoria sometimes get a reduction in the funeral costs and members of the Cremation Society are sometimes able to claim a reduction in fees.

Serving members of the armed forces

The Ministry of Defence will assist with the cost and type of funeral, the precise help given depending on the place of death, the type of funeral requested and the place where it is to take place.

War pensioners

If the deceased was a war pensioner who fulfilled certain conditions, a non-repayable grant to help with the cost of a basic funeral is available. Enquiry should be made of the War Pensions Agency.

The Social Fund

A partner or other person who reasonably assumed responsibility for a funeral in the absence of a partner or close relatives able to meet the cost, and who is receiving:

◆ Income Support or

◆ Income based Jobseeker's Allowance or

◆ Housing Benefit or

◆ Council Tax Benefit or

◆ Pension Credit or

◆ Child Tax Credit at a rate higher than the family element or

◆ Working Tax Credit for a disabled worker

can sometimes obtain a contribution towards the cost of the funeral from the Social Fund. Application must be made on form SF200 to the local social security office within three months of the date of the funeral.

Bank and building society accounts and National Savings
Unless the deceased had a joint bank account or the total value of the estate was less than £5,000, money in a clearing bank account will not normally be available to meet the cost of the funeral until a grant of probate of the will or letters of administration have been issued by a probate registry, but if there is pressure from the funeral director for payment, a building society account or National Savings investments can sometimes be used to pay the funeral bill before the grant has been issued. Enquiry should be made of the building society or the appropriate department of National Savings and Investments.

$$\left(5\right)$$

Bereavement and Other Social Security Benefits

The death of your spouse or registered civil partner will cause substantial changes in your financial situation and may give you entitlement to new social security benefits or affect existing benefits.

Both men and women whose husbands, wives or civil partners have died may be able to claim bereavement benefits which depend on individual circumstances, but the benefits cease if the claimant remarries, registers a new civil partnership or begins living with a new partner.

BEREAVEMENT PAYMENT AND BEREAVEMENT ALLOWANCE

◆ **Bereavement Payment**. You may be entitled to a single tax free payment known as a Bereavement Payment, if your spouse or registered civil partner was not entitled to a CAT. A State Retirement Pension based on his or her own contributions when he or she died or if you are under state pension age. The current pension age is 65 for men and 60 for women but during the period 2010 to 2020 the age for women will be gradually increased until it equals that for men. Bereavement Payment is based on your spouse's or your civil partner's National Insurance contributions. The claim for Bereavement Payment must be made within 12 months of the death unless there are exceptional circumstances.

- **Bereavement Allowance**. You may be entitled to a periodic payment known as a Bereavement Allowance for up to 52 weeks or until you reach state pension age, whichever period is the shorter. The amount of the payment is based in part upon your spouse's or civil partner's National Insurance contributions and in part upon your age when your spouse or civil partner dies. You must be aged at least 45 when the death occurs to make a successful claim. The claim should be made promptly, because the allowance will only be payable from the date of the claim and not from the date of the death if claimed after three months from the date of the death.

Only the higher of Bereavement Allowance and State Retirement Pension is payable, not both.

Even if your spouse or civil partner had made insufficient National Insurance contributions you may be able to claim Bereavement Payment and Bereavement Allowance if he or she died as the result of an industrial disease or accident at work.

There is one claim form for the above benefits which is obtainable from the local Benefits Agency, the address of which can be found in a telephone directory.

It must be remembered that Bereavement Payment and Bereavement Allowance are only payable in respect of those who were legally married or registered civil partners at the time of the death and that for benefit purposes, if you remarry, live with another as man and wife or civil partner, you cease to be a widow or widower or partner of a deceased civil partner as the case may be for the purposes of Bereavement Payment and Bereavement Allowance.

Whether you are employed or not does not affect your entitlement to bereavement benefits.

WIDOWED PARENT'S ALLOWANCE

This is a benefit paid by regular payments to widows, widowers or registered civil partners who are under state pension age. It is based in part upon the deceased spouse's or registered partner's National Insurance contribution record and in part upon their earnings. It is payable to those who are eligible for child benefit or pregnant with their registered civil partner's or spouse's child or one conceived by in vitro or artificial insemination.

Anyone who is pregnant may qualify for one of the following:

◆ Statutory Maternity pay from an employer

◆ Maternity Allowance from the social security system

◆ A Sure Start Maternity Grant from the Social Fund.

Enquire at the local Social Security Office or Jobcentre.

INCAPACITY BENEFIT

If you are incapable of work and under state retirement age you might be entitled to this benefit until you reach that age.

THE STATE RETIREMENT PENSION

If you are receiving the State Retirement Pension in your own right when your spouse or civil partner dies, you may be entitled to an increase in the pension, and if you are not receiving a State Retirement Pension, you may become entitled to one. In each case it depends upon your late spouse's or partner's contribution record. Enquire at the Benefits Office.

WAR WIDOW'S PENSION
War Widow's Pension is becoming increasingly rare as the years pass, but if obtainable it is a particularly valuable benefit in that it is tax-free. It may be payable if your parent, registered civil partner or husband was receiving certain benefits as a consequence of injuries received in a war or his death resulted from injuries suffered in war.

JOB SEEKER'S ALLOWANCE
After the bereavement you might feel that not only do you need more money but you also have more available time and are lonely. If you decide to seek work you should note that you might be able to claim Job Seeker's Allowance if you are over 18 and under state pension age, and you are capable of work which you are actively seeking and for which you are available. The benefit is claimable either on the basis of low income or National Insurance contributions.

WORKING TAX CREDIT
This is a means tested benefit administered by the Inland Revenue payable both to the employed and self employed who work at least 16 hours a week and are over the age of 16. It is payable to low earners and intended to make work financially attractive. It can be claimed online at www.inlandrevenue.gov.uk/taxcredits or through the Inland Revenue Helpline telephone 0845 300 3900 or textphone 0845 300 3909.

INCOME SUPPORT

Income support is a benefit payable to people aged between 16 and 60 who have limited savings and have a low income. It is intended for those people of limited means who cannot be expected to do a normal week's work, e.g. those who are sick or disabled or are voluntary carers. It is not available to those who work for more than 16 hours a week or have a partner who works for 24 hours or more a week or those with over £8,000.00 in savings.

SOCIAL FUND PAYMENTS

I have previously referred to assistance from the Social Fund with the cost of the funeral and Sure Start Maternity Grants. Other grants and loans which do not depend upon National Insurance contributions are also available from the Social Fund to help with expenses which are burdensome and non-recurring. Some, but not all, are dependent upon already being in receipt of Income Support or income-based Job Seeker's Allowance and some, but not all, have to be repaid. Those that are loans and not grants and have to be repaid are free of interest.

ASSISTANCE WITH CHILDREN

If you are left to care for a child or children remember Widowed Parent's Allowance mentioned above and also consider claiming Child Benefit which is a non-means tested benefit payable to those who contribute towards the financial cost of bringing up a child. The child need not be your child or living with you but must be:

◆ under the age of 16; or

◆ under the age of 18 and registered at the careers office for work; or

◆ under the age of 19 and following a full time course of study.

Only one person or partner can receive Child Benefit in respect of any child and if a person in receipt of the benefit dies the benefit ceases unless a new claim is made by another person. Claim forms can be obtained from the local social security office or Jobcentre or from the Child Benefit Office.

In addition to Child Benefit a person with a child to care for may be entitled to Child Tax Credit, a means tested benefit administered by the Inland Revenue which can be claimed:

◆ online;

◆ through the Inland Revenue Helpline (0845 300 3900);

◆ through the local Job Centre; or

◆ through the social security office.

Guardian's Allowance
The requirements to qualify for Guardian's Allowance are complex but it is not necessary to be a guardian in the strict legal sense to be entitled to the allowance and it might well be worth making a claim.

BENEFITS FROM LOCAL AUTHORITIES
In addition to the above benefits, if you are on a low income and pay rent you might be entitled to Housing Benefit from the local council, and if you are on a low income and pay council tax you might be entitled to Council Tax Benefit. These two benefits are means tested. Remember also that if the death leaves you living alone in your property you will be

entitled to a reduction of 25 per cent on your council tax bill, and the following people who may in fact be living with you are ignored for the purpose of deciding whether or not you are living alone:

◆ anyone under the age of 18;

◆ students and those in further education;

◆ student nurses;

◆ Youth Training trainees and apprentices;

◆ anyone who has severe mental problems;

◆ those other than partners who care for you if you have a disability and receive certain benefits;

◆ paid care workers who live in;

◆ members of the armed forces and certain international institutions.

Part 2

Winding up Money Matters

6

Who Can and Should Wind Up Money Matters?

IF THERE IS A WILL

When a person dies it is necessary for someone to wind up that person's estate, i.e. their money, possessions, property and debts, by collecting what the deceased person owns and is due to him, paying the debts including any inheritance tax and passing anything that remains to those entitled to it.

Who is entitled to wind up the estate depends upon whether or not the deceased has left a valid will or codicil appointing an executor who is still living. A codicil is a document separate from the will but which is similarly signed and completed and which adds to or amends the will. An executor is a person to whom the will or codicil gives the task of carrying out the will.

If it is thought that the deceased left a will or a codicil but it cannot be found amongst his effects please refer to the suggested checks that might be made and the circumstances in which proof of a missing will might be obtained which are set out in the next chapter on pages 78 and 79.

If a document is found it will be necessary to consider:

◆ whether the deceased had the necessary legal capacity to make a will when he purported to make it;

◆ whether the requisite formalities were complied with when the will was made;

◆ whether the will remains valid or whether it has been revoked;

◆ to what property the will relates; and

◆ the legal effect of the will.

Deciding what the legal effect of a will is and what it means is dealt with in Chapter 9 pages 119 to 130.

Capacity to make a will
To make a valid will the testator must have valid testamentary capacity. This means that in addition to being over the age of 18 (unless he was seaman at sea, or in the armed forces and on active military service), he must have:

◆ been able to understand roughly what making a will means, i.e. the nature of the transaction he was entering into;

◆ been capable of having a rough idea of what he had to leave;

◆ been aware of those he had a moral obligation to benefit and those he was benefiting in the will; and

◆ understood in broad terms the effect of the will.

The testator may have had testamentary capacity and been able to make a valid will even though he was of unsound mind and suffering from delusions in some respects, as long as that insanity did not affect the above points, for example he may have good testamentary capacity even though he was convinced that the world was a cube.

The will will not be invalid if the testator became totally insane or otherwise lost his testamentary capacity after making it, as long as he had testamentary capacity at the time it was made. Even if the testator was normally mentally incapable, he would be legally able to make a valid will in any lucid period.

In making the will the testator must have been acting of his own free will and not under duress or the undue influence of any other person.

If the will is rational on the face of it there is a rebutable presumption that the testator had full testamentary capacity and was making it of his own free will.

The formalities for making a valid will

Wills made outside England and Wales
If a will was made outside England and Wales English Law will accept its validity if it is made:

◆ in accordance with the formalities required by the state where it was made; or

◆ in accordance with the formalities required by the state where, at the time the will was made or at death, the testator was domiciled or had his habitual residence or of which he was a national.

A will made on a ship or in an aircraft will be treated as validly completed if it was completed in accordance with the law of the country with which the ship or aircraft has the closest connection.

Wills which deal with foreign property
If the will deals with immoveable property such as a holiday villa, it will be recognised as valid by English law if it complies with the formalities required by the law of the state in which the property is situated.

When considering the provisions of a will in respect of any foreign property the testator may have, it is also necessary to consider the foreign law relating to the property and the making of wills, even if the will is made in the United Kingdom. Some states have restrictions in relation to who can inherit property and the tax laws relating to property differ from those of English law. The procedure and formalities for making a will that is to be recognised by the foreign country as a valid document of title to the property are also usually different from those of England and Wales.

Wills made by a member of the armed forces engaged in actual military service or a seaman at sea
If the will is made by a member of the armed forces engaged in actual military service or a seaman at sea no formalities are required to be followed to make, or indeed to revoke, a will; their wills can be made irrespective of age, do not have to be in writing and if written do not need to be witnessed.

Other wills made in England or Wales
If a will made in England or Wales (other than the will of a member of the armed forces engaged in actual military service or a seaman at sea) is to be considered to be a valid will the following formalities must have been complied with:

- the will must be in writing. Any form of writing, handwritten, typed or printed and in any language will suffice, but it *must be in writing* and any other expression of wishes will not be effective. Oral expressions of the testator's wishes and wills recorded on sound-tapes or videotapes are therefore not valid wills. The will can be written *on any material*, on paper, parchment, linen or even carved in stone!

- the will must have been signed by the testator or by someone in his presence and at his request. The signature need not be the testator's full name or indeed his name at all as long as a court will be satisfied that the mark which was made was intended as the testator's signature and that it was intended to authenticate the document as his will.

- The testator's signature on the will must have been made or acknowledged by the testator in the presence of two or more witnesses who were present at the same time.

- Each witness must have signed the will and either signed or acknowledged his signature in the testator's presence.

- It must be apparent that the testator intended to give effect to the will by signing it. In practice the testator's signature and those of the witnesses usually appear at the end of the will to show that they are intended to give effect as the testator's will to all that goes before the signatures. If words appear in the will after the signatures of the testator there can be problems, in that the Probate Registry will insist upon the witnesses swearing an affidavit or making an affirmation to confirm that the words were in the will when it was signed and were not added later by the testator or by anyone else. If the words were added later of course, they would be ineffective and invalid and would not be admitted to probate.

Has the will or any part of it been revoked?

Revocation by marriage or civil partnership.
If a testator goes through a ceremony of marriage or registration of civil partnership after the date of a will, it will revoke the will unless the will expressly states that it is made with that particular marriage or partnership in mind and is to continue in force after the marriage or partnership. For the effect of a decree of divorce or annulment of marriage or dissolution of civil partnership on a will please refer to Chapter 9 pages 121 to 122.

Revocation by destruction with intention to revoke.
A will will have been revoked if it was destroyed by the testator or by another person at his request and in his presence. In either case the testator must have intended that the will should be revoked. The formalities must have been strictly followed. It is not sufficient that the word 'revoked' is written on the will or that part of the will has been crossed out. If the will is only partially destroyed or obliterated e.g. by tearing a piece out of the will, unless that piece is a vital part of the will, only the piece torn out or obliterated will have been revoked and the remainder of the will will still be valid. Neither is it sufficient if the will was accidentally destroyed, or if the testator was so drunk that he did not know what he was doing when he destroyed the will or if he otherwise lacked mental capacity. Moreover, if the testator asked someone to destroy his will for him, the destruction will have been ineffective unless it was done in his presence; for this purpose presence is narrowly interpreted and it is not sufficient if the person who destroyed the will did so in another room.

Revocation of a will by a new will or by a codicil
A new will or codicil which contains a clause to revoke an earlier will in its entirety, or to revoke only some of the provisions of the existing will is effective, but the new will or codicil must be signed and the testator's signature witnessed in accordance with the formalities for making a will or the revocation will not be effective.

Implied revocation
If there is a later will or codicil containing no revocation clause but containing provisions which are inconsistent with an earlier will, the provisions of the earlier will which are inconsistent with the later will are considered to be revoked, but the other provisions of the earlier will remain valid, as do all the provisions of the later will.

A later will or codicil containing no revocation clause or provisions which are inconsistent with an earlier will does not revoke the earlier will and both the earlier will and the later document are effective so far as they are not inconsistent. Thus it is possible that there will be more than one will valid at any given time.

The effect of obliterations, insertions or alterations in a will or codicil
Any alteration, insertion or obliteration in a will or codicil will be of no effect unless it has been signed by the testator, and his signature has been witnessed in the same way as is required for the completion of a will or codicil, or initialled first by the testator and then by the witnesses in the document near the alteration, obliteration or insertion. If the alterations are not signed or initialled in this way and the original writing is still legible, a court will give effect to the will in its unaltered form, but if the alterations are not so signed or initialled and the

original wording has been obliterated and is illegible, both the original and the altered wording will be ignored and the will will take effect as if there is a blank space in the will.

To what property does the will relate?
When considering the provisions of a will which has provisions (such as the appointment of an executor) in respect of any property the testator may have which is situated abroad, it is also necessary to consider the foreign law relating to the making of wills and the property, even if the will was made in the United Kingdom. The procedure and formalities for making a will that is to be recognised by the foreign country as a valid document of title to the property are different from those of England and Wales, and a lawyer who is qualified to practise in the foreign country should be consulted. The Law Society or relevant foreign embassy will be able to put you in touch with a suitable lawyer. Some states also have restrictions in relation to who can inherit property and the tax laws relating to property differ from those of English law.

If the deceased left a valid will or codicil that is relevant to property in England or Wales, the people with the first right to deal with or administer the estate are the executors appointed by the will or by a codicil, but if the appointed sole executor is under the age of eighteen, he cannot act, although the High Court can appoint his parent, guardian or another person to act for him until he becomes of age.

Even though a person has been named in a will as an executor, he is not obliged to act as executor. He can sign a form of renunciation (obtainable from law stationers) giving up the right to the executorship, provided that he does so before he exercises any of the rights or carries out any of the duties of an executor. If one appointed executor renounces executorship, the other appointed executors may proceed to obtain a grant of probate of the will.

An executor who wishes to renounce his right to probate, but cannot find his co-executor or the next person in line to prove the will or entitled to letters of administration of the estate, can discharge himself and obtain a receipt by lodging the renunciation document, together with the will or codicil at any District Probate Registry.

A further possibility is for an appointed executor to ask the Probate Registry to allow the other executors to go ahead and prove the will without him, without finally giving up his right to act as executor at a later stage should he later wish to do so. This is known as reserving power to prove a will and is particularly useful to cover the possibility that one of two executors might obtain probate alone but die before completing the winding up of the estate. The executor to whom probate has been reserved can then apply to the Probate Registry for authority to take over and finalise the administration and the winding up of the estate.

If all the executors are unable or unwilling to take on the work, or the will or codicil has not given anyone the position of executor, members of the following groups of people are entitled to apply for a grant of representation:

1. The person, or people, to whom the deceased has left the entirety of his estate.

2. The person entitled to that part of the estate which remains after taking out any specific gifts or legacies made by the will, or if they survived the testator but died without taking out a grant of representation, their personal representatives.

3. Specific legatees or creditors of the estate.

4. The Crown.

Only when there is no member of a group who is willing to take out a grant will a member of the next group be considered.

IF THERE IS IS NO VALID WILL

If there is no valid will, the following are entitled to wind up the estate, and again only when there is no member of a group who is willing to take out a grant will a member of the next group be considered:

1. Husband or wife or registered civil partner.

2. Sons or daughters, or their descendants if the son or daughter died before the deceased.

3. Parents.

4. Brothers or sisters of the whole blood, or their descendants if the brother or sister died before the deceased.

5. Brothers or sisters of the half blood, or their descendants if the brother or sister died before the deceased.

6. Grandparents.

7. Uncles or aunts of the whole blood, or their descendants if the uncle or aunt died before the deceased.

8. Uncles or aunts of the half blood, or their descendants if the uncle or aunt died before the deceased.

9. The crown.

10. Creditors of the deceased.

All those within each group are equally entitled, but only blood and adoptive relationships count, not step relations. Adoption severs the relationship between parent and child for this purpose but illegitimacy is ignored, and legitimate and illegitimate claimants have equal rights.

If the beneficiaries include someone entitled to a life interest or beneficiary under the age of eighteen, at least two people from the above categories must jointly obtain the right to wind up the estate from the probate registry.

THE GRANT OF REPRESENTATION

To prove a right to wind up an estate one obtains, i.e. 'takes out' from a probate registry, a document called **probate** if one is an executor appointed by the will or codicil or **letters of administration of the estate** in any other case. Both probate and letters of administration are sometimes referred to as the grant of representation and those to whom they are granted are sometimes referred to as Personal Representatives.

Except where a minimum of two are required as specified above, any number up to four of the people within each group specified above or any four executors may take out the grant together, but people from different groups may not be mixed. If the applicant is proposing to take out the grant on behalf of someone who is out of the country, or if the beneficiaries include an infant or beneficiary lacking legal mental capacity, a guarantee from a bank or insurance company is required.

To have entitlement to wind up an estate a person must also be of full age, not bankrupt and of sound mind.

SHOULD ONE EMPLOY A SOLICITOR OR DEAL WITH THE ESTATE ONESELF?

Each course has its advantages and disadvantages.

The main advantages of employing a solicitor are:

◆ If the terms of the will are contentious or not clear, the solicitor who is trained in the law and experienced in these matters should be able to give sound guidance.

◆ In the event of a mistake being made as a result of his negligence, the solicitor will be insured to cover any claims by the executor or the beneficiaries including the cost of properly pursuing the claims.

◆ In the event of unsatisfactory work or overcharging by solicitors complaints may be made to The Law Society Consumer Complaints Service. However, its idea of what constitutes fair and reasonable fees or unsatisfactory work might not be the same as the complainant's and the process is laborious and slow.

◆ Much of the burden of the routine work involved will be taken over by the solicitor, although it will still be necessary for the personal representative to spend a great deal of time having meetings with, telephoning and writing letters to the solicitor, searching out documents, signing authorities, receipts, transfer documents and withdrawal forms.

◆ If the personal representative is a close friend or relative of the deceased, everything the personal representative does in relation to the estate will be a reminder and perhaps prove upsetting.

The main advantage of the DIY approach is:

◆ Cost saving – solicitors' businesses are expensive to run and, as most people will know, their fees are not cheap, although few who have not experienced employing a solicitor in a probate matter will realise how expensive this can be.

Let me explain by way of an example.

The usual practice in probate matters is for a solicitor to charge a fee based on the time spent in carrying out the work, the fee being known as the hourly rate (i.e. charge per hour). In addition, a solicitor will frequently charge fees based on a percentage of the value of the gross estate.

The hourly rate depends upon the individual solicitor's proportion of the cost of running the practice and the seniority of the person doing the work. Typical hourly rates at the present time might be between £85 and £200.

The percentage charge is usually between 1 per cent and 2 per cent.

Even more might be charged if unusually complex legal points arise.

In 2003 The Court of Appeal reviewed the basis upon which solicitors should be allowed to decide upon charges in probate matters in the case of Jemma Trust Co v Liptrott and Others, and confirmed that solicitors employed in the administration of an estate are entitled to charge both on the basis of an hourly rate and in addition a percentage of the value of the estate, as long as the total bill is 'fair and reasonable remuneration taking all relevant factors into account', and as long as the value element was not also taken into account in the calculation of the hourly rate and charged twice.

The following bands and rates for the value element were considered as likely to be reasonable:

(a) up to £1 million – $1^1/_2$ per cent (one and a half per cent) of the gross estate

(b) £1 million–£4 million – $^1/_2$ per cent of the gross estate

(c) £4 million–£8 million – $^1/_6$ per cent of the gross estate

(d) £8 million–£12 million – $^1/_{12}$ per cent of the gross estate.

The bands were only to be used as a guideline and were not to be regarded as sacrosanct. The Court also suggested that at the end of the work, if solicitors seek to charge in part on a value element, it might be helpful also to calculate the number of hours that would notionally be taken to achieve the separate charge to determine whether the overall remuneration was fair and reasonable.

The court considered that an hourly rate calculated on the basis of the expense rate (i.e. the cost to the solicitor of running his share of his practice) plus 25–33 per cent of that cost was too low if a value element was not also included.

Suppose someone dies leaving an estate consisting of, say:

◆ a freehold house valued at £180,000;

◆ furniture and personal effects of £15,000;

- life insurance policies £10,000;

- balance at the bank £300;

- savings with two building societies totalling £8,000;

- an ISA value £12,000;

- Premium Bonds £700;

- Pensioners Bonds £2,000;

- cash £100;

- shares made up of four different holdings totalling £5,900.

Suppose also there are three beneficiaries and two non-professional executors. A solicitor's fee for the work to be done would probably be calculated as follows:

1 ½ per cent of the value of the gross estate	£3,510.00
Hourly rate charge: 14 hours at £100 per hour	£1,400.00
Total fee exclusive of VAT	£4,910.00
Add VAT at 17.5 per cent of £4,910	£859.25
Total bill saved on this estate if no solicitor is employed	£5,769.25

In the Jemma Trust case the court suggested solicitors should obtain the prior agreement of the executors and the residuary beneficiaries as to what the basis of their charges would be. In order to make future charges transparent the Law Society requires solicitors to enter into a written 'Client Agreement' with the client; this sets out at the beginning of the transaction the basis upon which the charge for the work to be done shall be calculated.

If pressed, most solicitors will reluctantly agree a fixed fee for probate transactions at the outset rather than lose the business.

◆ The personal representative is much more in control of the pace at which the winding up of the estate progresses and is fully aware of the situation at all times. Most solicitors work under great pressure and do not find the time to chase up a tardy reply. Unless carried out by someone who does no other work than probate work, the probate files tend to get put on one side and take second priority to court work and conveyancing where there are strict time limits with disastrous consequences if the time limits are not met. Moreover, most solicitors are notoriously bad at keeping the client informed of progress or lack of progress.

A solicitor should be consulted immediately if:

◆ the estate looks as though it is likely to be too small to pay all the debts and legacies; or

◆ claims are made against the estate or the personal representative's handling of it; or

◆ the personal representative is unsure about any point; or

◆ trusts or foreign property are involved; or

◆ the inheritance tax bill is large and there might be the possibility of reducing it by claiming reliefs such as business relief, agricultural property relief or woodland relief or rearranging the entitlements to the estate by means of a deed of family arrangement.

A solicitor will be able to give advice on a specific point or on the administration of the estate generally.

7

Winding up an Estate Yourself – Proving Your Right to Act

JOINTLY OWNED PROPERTY

There are two ways of owning property jointly in English law, namely as joint tenants or as tenants in common. The use of the word 'tenants' has nothing to do with tenants in the sense of landlord and tenant: it is merely the same word used as a technical term to signify a different concept.

If people own property as joint tenants the law provides that on the death of one joint owner, that person's share of the jointly owned property does not become part of his estate (except for Inheritance Tax purposes), does not fall to be dealt with by his personal representatives and is inherited by the surviving joint owners regardless of the terms of the deceased's will or the circumstances of his intestacy. On the other hand, if people own property as tenants in common, the law provides that on the death of one joint owner that person's share of the jointly owned property does becomes part of his estate, falls to be dealt with by his personal representatives and is inherited as provided for in his will, if there is one, or if none, then by his next of kin in accordance with the intestacy laws.

It follows therefore that if property is owned as joint tenants, all that is necessary for the survivor to prove a right to deal with the property and to inherit it, is to produce satisfactory evidence of death, i.e. a death certificate, or an order of a court giving leave to presume death.

On the other hand if property is owned as tenants in common, the person claiming the right to deal with the deceased's share as executor of a will must prove that he is the executor appointed by a valid will or codicil, and if there is no will or a will but no executor appointed or willing to prove it, other proof must be given of the right to deal with the deceased's share of the jointly owned property.

The document evidencing proof that the will is a valid one is called probate of the will or, if there is no validly appointed executor who is willing to prove it, or all the appointed executors have died before the person who made the will, it is called letters of administration.

If no valid will exists the next of kin must obtain a different document (also confusingly called letters of administration) to prove the right to deal with the deceased's assets including any share of jointly owned property which was held as tenants in common.

Grants of probate and letters of administration are sometimes conveniently referred to as the grant of representation and the way they are obtained is described on pages 76 to 99.

How does one know whether jointly owned property was held as joint tenants or tenants in common? Usually bank and building society accounts and stocks and shares are held in joint tenancies, but if there is any evidence to show that the joint owners owned separate shares of the property as opposed to each joint owner owning the entirety, the joint ownership is a case of tenancies in common. Joint tenants always own the asset equally and words indicating that the joint owners own unequally always mean a tenancy in common. Partnerships almost invariably own property as tenants in common. When husbands and wives own property jointly they usually, but not necessarily, do so as joint tenants and not tenants in common.

IF THE GROSS ESTATE IS VALUED UNDER £15,000
If the value of the estate before deducting the cost of the funeral and any debts left by the deceased is under £15,000, it is frequently worth writing to the bodies which hold the assets, to ask that they make payment to the personal representative without the necessity of going to the expense of obtaining a grant of representation and what their requirements are to enable this to be done.

Provided there is not more than £5,000 (and sometimes £15,000) the bank or building society etc will usually make payment to those entitled in return for the sight of the original will, or if there is no will, in return for a short statement as to the identity and relationship of the next of kin. In each case the registrar's death certificate must be produced and a short form of indemnity which the bank or building society will prepare must be signed.

IF THE GROSS ESTATE IS VALUED OVER £15,000
If the value of the estate before deducting the cost of the funeral and any debts left by the deceased is over £5,000 (or sometimes £15,000), then before the assets of the estate can be dealt with, probate of the will or letters of administration must be obtained.

The procedure to be followed is essentially the same in the case of both probate and letters of administration.

There are three main steps involved:

1. obtaining the information necessary to prepare the papers to obtain the grant of representation;

2. preparing and lodging the documentation to obtain inheritance tax assessment and the issue of the grant of representation; and

3. registering the grant in connection with the various assets and giving instructions as to how they are to be dealt with, e.g. transferred to a person entitled on the death, sold or cashed and collecting what is due to the estate.

Following the completion of the above three steps to finally wind up the money side one must:

◆ finalise the income and capital gains tax positions;

◆ pay off the debts and discharge the liabilities of the estate; and

◆ distribute the remaining assets of the estate to those who are entitled to them (who are called the beneficiaries).

Each step is separately explained below and appendices contain appropriate drafts for most of the letters that will need to be written and useful addresses.

OBTAINING THE NECESSARY INFORMATION TO PREPARE THE PAPERS TO OBTAIN THE GRANT OF REPRESENTATION

Is there a valid will?
If a document is found which is believed to be a will its validity and effect should be considered in the light of the

requirements set out in the later section dealing with interpreting a will on pp 119–130. It is now unusual to 'read' a will to the family, but if relatives wish to know the contents of the will no harm will be done by supplying them with a copy rather than causing ill feeling by refusing to do so, because once the will has been proved, anyone interested can obtain a copy from the Probate Registry for a nominal fee.

If it is believed that the deceased made a will but the will cannot be found it may well have been lodged with the deceased's solicitor, bank or accountant for safe-keeping. If they have no knowledge of it enquire of the Record Keeper's Department at Principal Probate Registry with whom wills can be deposited for safe-keeping (contact details can be found in Appendix 2 Useful Addresses). The Registry keeps an index of wills which is searched every time an application is made for a grant of representation to an estate. Also check the internet website *www.1st.locate.co.uk* where it is possible to register the existence of a will and where it is to be found. Even if a will has found there could be later wills in existence and so a thorough search must be made.

If all else fails it is sometimes possible to prove a will by a copy or reconstructed will (or in very exceptional circumstances even by oral evidence) if the original has been accidentally destroyed or lost.

To prove a will if it has been lost or accidentally destroyed there must be reasonable evidence both that the will was properly made and what its contents were. As Lord Justice Jacobs said in the case of Parks v Clout in 2003, the formalities set out in the Wills Act 'do really matter. One must have a reasonably firm basis for concluding that the formalities were carried out, not merely what the substance of the will was.' Hearsay evidence is admissible to prove the existence or otherwise of a will, and the existence and contents of a will can be proved by circumstantial evidence, but there must still be reasonable evidence of both the existence of the will and what its contents were, and also that it has not been validly revoked. If the missing will is last known to have been in the testator's possession there is a presumption that he destroyed it with the intention of revoking it but the presumption can be rebutted. In the recent case of Rowe v Clarke concerning a substantial estate, the presumption was held to have been rebutted by evidence of the long standing and continuing close friendship of the testator (who was a disorganised alcoholic) with the will beneficiary and the lack of contact between the testator and the person who would have inherited if the testator was found to have died intestate. The required standard of proof that the will was completed in accordance with the formal requirements of the Wills Act and of what its contents were is a balance of probabilities, and the burden of proof is upon the person who seeks to uphold the document as a valid will. A higher standard of proof is required to prove fraudulent behaviour such as fraudulent destruction of a will.

THE ASSETS AND LIABILITIES OF THE ESTATE

It is useful to start by making a list of everything the deceased had which can be turned into money (whether or not sale is intended) and to list all the known debts. This list can be used as a worksheet and can be used to record information which will be required to prepare the papers which are necessary to obtain the grant of representation, and to track progress in the administration of the estate, thus showing at a glance what has been done and what remains to be done at any time. An example of a suitable form of worksheet is set out in Appendix 1.

Sometimes it is difficult to discover exactly what assets a person leaves. If this is not known, a search of the home for papers will usually give clues. Besides safes and filing cabinets, many people use furniture drawers, bureaux and wardrobes to store (and hide!) their papers. I have even come across building society passbooks kept in the refrigerator (hot money?) and cash hidden on a ledge inside a disused fireplace, as well as cash under floorboards, carpets and a bed mattress. Safe and other keys are often hidden behind books on bookshelves.

Bank statements show direct payments into the account such as pension payments and share dividends. If a dividend has been received the company registrar will be able to confirm the holding. The registrar's address appears on the tax certificates attached to dividend warrants if any can be found. Do not forget that a company's website will also yield the company registrar's address. Sometimes the registrar's website will reveal the holding, although one will need the deceased's password to obtain details of the holding from the website.

Bank statements will also give a clue to regular outgoings.

If it is suspected there might be a bank or building society account but details are sparse, try completing and submitting a dormant account form obtainable from any bank or building society branch respectively.

Occupational and insured pension schemes must register and update their registered particulars annually. Following acquisitions, mergers and company insolvencies schemes may have changed their names. To trace suspected pension entitlements from former employers, try submitting a Pensions Trace Request Form (obtainable from some post offices or from the Department for Work and Pensions) to The Pensions Tracing Service at The Department for Work and Pensions or the Pensions Regulator. The tracing service is free.

The British Bankers Association and the Building Societies Association may be able to help where there have been mergers, takeovers or changes in the names of member institutions.

National Savings and Investments runs a scheme to trace possible accounts, certificates and premium bond prizes and a National Savings Tracing Service application form can be obtained from Freepost BJ2092, Blackpool FY3 9YP, or by telephoning 0845 964 5000.

Since the Financial Services and Marketing Act 2000 came into force on 1 December 2001, the Financial Services Authority is responsible for regulating all deposit, insurance and investment business in this country and has taken over a vast number of records. The Authority maintains a Register of Firms which can be very useful and might be able to help in tracing changes in friendly societies and insurance companies.

Enquiry can also be made of the deceased's solicitors, bank, accountant, stockbroker and other financial advisers for the will and required financial information. Even if one has found a will there could be later wills in existence.

When making the list care should be taken to include only items that belong to the deceased in the estate and to exclude items which are on hire or hire purchase. Library items or NHS equipment, such as wheelchairs, artificial aids or limbs, should not be included and should be returned.

Television and motor car licences, season tickets and membership documents in respect of associations and clubs and any items which are on hire or hire purchase should be returned promptly in case it is possible to obtain a refund of fees.

When the list is more or less complete, steps should be taken to obtain a figure for the value of each asset and the amount of each debt or other liability and the appropriate figure should be entered on the list. A value as at the date of death must be obtained for every asset and liability of the estate before a grant of representation to the estate can be obtained. The value required for inheritance tax purposes and to obtain a grant of representation to an estate is the open market value as at the date of death, i.e. the price that the item could reasonably be expected to obtain if sold on the open market as at the date of death. If the death occurred on a non-trading day such as a Sunday, the lower of the preceding or next trading days may be used. Care should be taken when choosing a lower valuation with a view to minimising inheritance tax because the inheritance tax valuation will become the base value for capital gains tax when the asset is subsequently sold in the course of administration of the estate or transferred to a beneficiary, and could thus increase any capital gains tax liability.

Bank and building society accounts
Each bank or building society should be written to at an early stage with a copy of the death certificate and most will also require sight of the original or a photostat copy of the will. A statement of the balance standing to the credit of each account including accrued interest as at the date of death should be obtained and if there is a passbook it should be enclosed to be made up to date.

The addresses can usually be obtained from the passbooks (if any), from old account statements, telephone directories, or on the society's website on the Internet.

The bank or building society will freeze the account and stop making standing orders and meeting direct debits when notified of the death. Cheques that have been drawn by the deceased but not presented for payment at that date will not be met.

Employment benefits

If the deceased was in employment at the date of death the employer should be written to in order to ascertain whether there are arrears of wages or any other benefits due to the estate at the date of death. The employer should also be asked to give useful information such as the address of the relevant tax district and tax reference of the deceased and the same information as to any pension scheme trustees. The trustees of the pension scheme should be asked to supply information as to whether there are any, and if so what, benefits due from the pension scheme and whether such benefits fall to be included in the estate for inheritance tax purposes.

If the deceased had changed employment or retired and there is difficulty in tracing the trustees of a pension scheme the Pension Regulator might be able to help.

Furniture and personal effects

The deceased's items of furniture, personal assets and effects and his share of any such jointly owned items must have a value attributed to them but they need not be individually valued. Usually a fair estimate of their total value is sufficient, but a professional valuation should be obtained from an auctioneer or valuer if they are not the usual run-of-the-mill items and it is suspected that they may be of significant value.

Most valuers charge for valuation on a time basis. A cursory viewing might cost £100 plus VAT but a more detailed inventory and valuation will cost more.

When valuables are removed from the deceased's premises remember to ensure that they are insured and adequately insured in the premises to which they are taken.

PEPs, ISAs TESSAs and unit trusts

The managers of PEPs, ISAs, TESSAs and any unit trust holding must be written to for a valuation of the holding as at the date of death unless the valuation can be obtained from prices quoted in the press.

If the death occurred on a non-trading day such as a Sunday, the lower of the preceding or next trading days can be used.

Unit trusts, unlike OEICS (open-ended investment company shares), have two prices: one at which the manager is prepared to sell the units and a lower price at which he is prepared to buy back the units. Unit trusts are valued for inheritance tax and probate purposes at the lower of the two prices.

Stocks and shares quoted on a recognised stock exchange

Likewise stocks and shares have two prices – a buying price and a selling price – and if the death occurred on a non-trading day such as a Sunday, the lower of the preceding or next trading days may be used.

The price quoted in the press as the closing price on any day is usually a middle price, half way between the closing buying and selling prices.

The proper way of valuing stocks and shares for inheritance tax and probate purposes is to work out two figures and to use the lower figure. The first figure is obtained by adding to the lower closing price for the day a quarter of the difference between the buying and the selling price. The second figure is the figure which is midway between the highest and the lowest recorded price for the relevant day. For a small fee The London Stock Exchange Historic Price Service, which can be consulted on its website www.londonstockexchange.com/en-gb/products or in writing, will supply the final prices for the relevant day for any quoted security and if the security was quoted ex-dividend the dividend rate per share. The current fee can be obtained by telephoning, e-mailing or faxing the service. Alternatively valuations of stocks or shares for probate purposes can be obtained from most stockbrokers, a bank or from www.sharedata.co.uk (please refer to its website), but they do charge for the service and it might be wise to ask for an indication of the likely fee in advance.

If a share is quoted 'ex dividend', the dividend which has been declared must be included in the inheritance tax valuation of the estate: if loan or debenture stock is quoted ex interest then the interest less tax at the appropriate rate (currently 20 per cent) must be included.

Unquoted stocks and shares

Any securities such as shares or loan or debenture stock which are not quoted on a recognised stock exchange are valued according to the percentage of the company's share capital held by the deceased. Thus a shareholding of 50 per cent or less is valued on the basis of the dividend yield, a holding of between 50 per cent and 90 per cent is valued on the basis of earnings yield, and a holding of over 90 per cent upon an assets basis. The value will eventually have to be agreed by the Inland Revenue Shares Valuation Division, but the easiest way for the layman to get an initial figure is to ask the company secretary for a figure, or if the deceased owned only a small percentage of the company's shares, to ask the secretary at what price dealings, if any, last took place and to use that price.

Life and endowment policies

For these policies, write to the company concerned and try to deal with head office rather than the local office. The head office address usually appears on the policy document, but it might not be the latest address and the company name may have changed. In that event it might be necessary to visit the company's website or, if the name has changed, to enquire of the Financial Services Authority or the British Insurance Association.

The value of a policy which matures on the death of the deceased is the amount paid out by the assurance company. If the policy is one that matures on the death of another person, the inheritance tax value is what it can be sold for, i.e. its open market value, and not its surrender value which will usually be less.

If the policy was taken out by another person on the life of the deceased or taken out by the deceased expressly upon trust for another person, it will not form part of the deceased's estate and the insurance company will make payment to the person who took it out, or upon whose behalf it was taken out, as the case may be, upon production of the policy and a death certificate without the necessity of waiting for a grant of representation to be obtained.

National Savings products
Government stock on the old National Savings Bank Register
or the Bank of England Register is valued on the same basis as
other stock exchange quoted stock or quoted shares.
Government Stock is sometimes known as 'Gilts' and the
registrar who administers the stock on behalf of the
government is Computershare Investor Services Plc. whose
contact details are set out in the appendix.

Valuations for other National Savings products can be
obtained by writing to the Director of Savings at the address
given in Appendix 2 for the relevant product.

Benefits from the State
If the deceased was in receipt of any such benefit, e.g.
unemployment, retirement or widow's benefit or income
support, the Pension Service should be contacted quoting the
deceased's National Insurance number and the position as to
any arrears or overpaid benefit established. The address of the
Pension Service can be obtained from the local telephone
directory.

Land and buildings
For houses and other land or buildings, talk to a local estate
agent who might be prepared to give an opinion of the value
for probate purposes, especially if he thinks that it might lead
to a sale. Again ask if there will be a charge and if so how
much. Do not ask for a formal valuation, which could be very
expensive indeed, but for an opinion of the market price
current as at the date of death.

As a last resort, ask yourself at what price you would have
been prepared to sell the property.

Valuations for probate should be an accurate representation of the open market sale price as at the date of death because they will have to be sworn to by the personal representative, but when all is said and done, values are a matter of opinion unless the matter is tested by an actual sale and opinions differ.

If the Revenue disagrees with the personal representative's valuation, he can always concede gracefully to the Revenue's superior and better informed opinion and no harm will have been done, as long as the value originally suggested was not so far out as to be viewed as an obvious attempt to defraud the Revenue. If the Revenue does not challenge, a goodly sum of money might be saved by a fair and knowledgeable amateur valuation! If the Revenue does challenge the valuation and the personal representative cannot agree the Revenue's valuation, an appeal can be made to the Lands Tribunal or on a point of law to the High Court, but such appeals are costly and might well be unsuccessful. The Inland Revenue Stamp Duty Office informs the Local District Valuer of the price at which every sale in the Valuer's district takes place and so the District Valuer is well informed on such matters.

In the following two cases, where there is the possibility of claiming a deduction, the services of a professional should be sought.

In the case of jointly owned land or buildings, when they are held as tenants in common, the Revenue will frequently allow a deduction of 10 per cent of the market value to reflect the fact that few would wish to buy a share of a property in which they could only share occupation with a stranger or incur the expense of forcing a sale. The deduction is not allowed if the joint owners are husband and wife or if the property was owned as joint tenants and the capital gains tax implications of claiming the deduction should be carefully considered.

If it can be proved that although the land or buildings are in the sole name of the deceased, in fact another who claims shared ownership and whose name does not appear on the title provided part of the purchase price, the inheritance tax valuation can reflect that situation. This situation usually arises if a parent or child has helped the other to acquire a property.

If the land or buildings are mortgaged, the full value unmortgaged should be included and the amount outstanding on the mortgage should be included separately as a liability of the estate. The mortgage might be supported by a whole life or endowment policy lodged as collateral security for the mortgage debt, in which case a value for the policy will also have to be obtained and the policy proceeds included in the probate papers as a separate asset.

Interests in trusts

If the deceased was entitled to income from a trust, the proportion of the value of the trust's assets, assessed in the same fraction as the income to which the deceased was entitled bears to the entire income of the trust, is included in the deceased's estate for inheritance tax purposes. Thus if the deceased was entitled to one quarter of the income of the trust, then one quarter of the value of the trust's assets (valued as described above) must be included in the value of the deceased's estate, even if the deceased was only entitled to that income during his lifetime. In the case of a discretionary trust, no potential beneficiary is *entitled* to income or capital from the trust; income and capital are allocated to the potential beneficiaries *in the trustees' discretion* or accumulated within the trust and the death of a potential beneficiary does not give rise to a charge to inheritance tax.

Income and capital gains taxes

The Inspector of Taxes who dealt with the deceased's tax matters should be notified of the death and enquiry should be made as to the standing of the deceased's tax affairs to ascertain the amount of tax outstanding or refunds of overpaid tax due to the estate.

Which tax office is the appropriate tax office depends upon the particular circumstances of the deceased. If the deceased had a pension from a former employer or was employed when he died, the pension payer or the employer will be able to supply the name and address of the relevant tax district and the tax reference: if the deceased was self employed, try the tax office nearest to the main place of business, and if the deceased was not in employment and had no occupational pension, contact the tax office closest to the home address. The addresses of tax offices can be found in telephone directories under Inland Revenue.

It will be necessary to complete final tax returns up to the date of death. It should also be mentioned at this stage that, before finally distributing the estate between those entitled to it, it will also be necessary to complete final tax returns and settle any outstanding tax due in relation to income received between death and final distribution.

The deceased is entitled to a full year's tax allowances for the portion of the tax year in which he died and is frequently entitled to an income tax refund when the tax due to the date of death has been calculated. Tax credits on dividend income are not refundable. Any tax refund is an asset of the estate and

must be included in the papers for inheritance tax and probate
but there is no necessity to delay application for probate until
the Revenue has agreed the precise figure; an estimate is
accepted if it is described as such and adjusted later when the
precise figure is known.

If the period of administration covers several tax years, a
separate return will be required for each tax year or part of a
tax year. Income received in respect of a period up to and after
the date of death is not apportioned; which tax return it is
entered into depends upon the date it is paid or due to be paid
and not the period over which it accrues. It should be noted
that no capital gains tax liability arises by reason of the death,
as opposed to liability for tax on gains arising on disposals by
the deceased during his lifetime or by the personal
representatives during the administration of the estate. Capital
losses incurred by the deceased during his lifetime but in the
year of his death may be carried back and set against net gains
made in the three tax years preceding the tax year in which the
deceased died. For capital gains tax purposes the beneficiaries
of an estate are deemed to acquire assets transferred to them at
their value as at the date of death.

Debts and liabilities

If the deceased was in receipt of a pension (either state or
private) or National Insurance benefits, the payers should be
written to with a copy of the death certificate to enquire as to
any sums underpaid or overpaid and repayable.
Underpayments must be included in the documents to be
prepared to lead to the issue of the grant of representation as
assets of the estate, and overpayments may be included as
debts and deducted from the value of the estate for inheritance
tax purposes, thus reducing the amount of any inheritance tax
which will have to be paid.

Any mortgagees should be notified of the death promptly, as should the local authority for local government tax purposes, the suppliers of meals on wheels, any carers, the suppliers of gas, electricity, telephone, internet, cable or satellite TV services and any body with which the deceased had credit, debit or store cards. They should each be asked for the amount due to the date of death and they and all other known creditors should be requested to withhold any action contemplated to recover the debts until a grant of representation can be obtained and the estate put in funds.

If one-third of the purchase price of goods on hire purchase has been paid they cannot be repossessed without a court order.

In the case of credit, debit and store cards, if the beneficiaries of the estate have the requisite funds, they may wish to pay off any outstanding funds to avoid interest charges accruing.

If the proposed personal representatives are not also the sole beneficiaries of the estate and are not sure that they know of all the debts, or are not certain that the deceased did not make a later will, or if they are not sure that they know all the relatives, they may wish to protect themselves by publishing a statutory advertisement for creditors pursuant to section 27 of the Trustee Act 1925. The advertisement should be published in *The London Gazette* and in a newspaper circulating in the area in which the deceased had a house or other land or lived. The broad effect of the publication of such notices is that anyone who reads the notice, but does not notify the personal representatives of a claim within two months of publication of the notice, is barred from claiming a debt or an entitlement under any later will or upon intestacy from the personal representatives after the estate has been distributed, unless the proposed representatives had notice of the debt from other sources. However, such claimants can still recover the debt from the beneficiaries.

A suitable form of notice appears in Appendix 1 and it should be noted that although local newspapers will usually accept such notices for publication before a grant of representation has been issued, the *London Gazette* has its own form of notice and will not accept the notice for publication from private individuals until a grant of representation is to hand.

If it is found that the debts and liabilities of the estate (including the funeral expenses and the cost of administering the estate) are likely to exceed the value of the estate's assets, a solicitor should be consulted immediately because the law prescribes an order of priority for payment in these circumstances, and if the personal representative does not adhere strictly to the order he may well find himself personally responsible for making good the losses of any who lose out. Indeed, in the case of an insolvent estate it might be better to formally renounce the right to administer the estate.

PREPARING AND LODGING THE DOCUMENTATION TO HAVE INHERITANCE TAX ASSESSED AND TO OBTAIN THE GRANT OF REPRESENTATION

The forms which have to be completed to obtain a grant of representation to the estate are a form which gives details of the deceased and of the applicants to the Probate Registry, and a form of account with supplementary pages which gives details of the value of the estate to the Capital Taxes Office. An applications pack including the form and advice leaflets can be obtained from The Personal Applications Section of The Probate Registry and the necessary forms to deal with inheritance tax can be obtained by telephoning the Inland Revenue Capital Taxes answerphone service on 0845 234

1020. Probate application forms can also be downloaded from the Court Service website www.courtservice.gov.uk and inheritance tax forms from the Capital Taxes Office website www.hmrc.gov.uk/cto. There are local probate offices in different parts of the country but in the event of difficulty write to:

> Probate Department
> The Principal Registry
> Family Division
> First Avenue House
> 42–49 High Holborn
> London WC1V 6NP

There are two types of inheritance tax account. The simpler form IHT205 is sufficient unless the total value (before deduction of debts and funeral expenses) of the deceased's assets, including his share of jointly owned assets and the assets of any trust fund from which he had a right to benefit, together with the value of any gifts made by him in the 7 years before his death, exceeds £285,000. If it does exceed £285,000, form IHT200 must be used.

With the forms the Probate Registry and The Capital Taxes Office will send a guide to completing the forms and a note as to where and at what stage they should be returned and what is to be returned with them. There should be no difficulty in completing the forms if the procedures outlined above have been followed and the relevant information obtained. When the necessary forms have been filled in and signed by those applying for the grant, the Probate Registry's form PA1 and the simpler form IHT205 or the probate summary form D18 should be returned to the Registry with one of the copy death certificates obtained when registering the death, the originals of any will and codicils and the fee for the application. If it has been necessary to complete form IHT200 instead of form IHT 205 it should not be sent to the Probate Registry, but retained for dispatch to the Capital Taxes Office after the Probate Registry has had an opportunity to peruse the papers and interview the applicants as explained later.

The District Probate Registries have local sub-offices at which applicants may choose to be interviewed but the papers should be sent to a District Registry and not to the local sub-office.

It is of the utmost importance to note that under no circumstances should any fastenings be removed from or anything ever be attached to a will or codicil in any way, even with a paperclip.

It is wise to keep a photostat copy of any will or codicil and it might also be useful to keep a photostat of any other documents sent to the probate registry, if this can be done without too much inconvenience.

After the Registry has read the documents, the applicants for the grant will be invited to attend at the Registry or a local probate office of their choice, by appointment, to affirm or swear on oath that the information which they have given is true. The attendance at the Registry also gives the applicants and the Registry an opportunity to deal with any matters which need to be clarified on either side. The applicants should take with them some form of identification and the documents and letters used to complete the application forms so that they can be checked. At the interview the probate summary form D18 is returned to the applicants and if it has been necessary to complete form IHT200 both this form and form D18 should be sent to the Capital Taxes Office. The Capital Taxes Office will then inform the applicants of the amount of inheritance tax it provisionally assesses as due and payable at that stage. Inheritance tax is normally due and payable when the applicants submit the form of account of the deceased's estate to the Revenue or on the date which is six months from the last day of the month in which the death occurred, if the form has still not been submitted by that date. For example if the deceased died on 5 January and the applicants submitted the form of account to the Capital Taxes Office on 8 May, any inheritance tax will become due and payable on 8 May; if the form of account is not submitted to the Revenue until 15 September the tax will become due and payable on 31 July being six months following the last day of the month in which the deceased died i.e. six months after 31 January.

In respect of the following assets the tax can be paid by ten equal annual instalments, the first instalment becoming payable six months after the death or at the time the grant of representation is applied for, whichever is the earlier:

◆ land and buildings;

◆ growing timber;

◆ the net value of a business or an interest in a business as an entirety, as contrasted with individual assets of the business;

◆ controlling shareholdings in a company whether or not it is a quoted company;

◆ holdings of unquoted shares whose minimum value is at least £20,000 and which represent at least 10 per cent of the company's issued share capital or if they are ordinary shares, 10 per cent of the company's issued ordinary share capital;

◆ holdings of unquoted shares in respect of which the tax cannot be paid in a single payment without undue hardship;

◆ holdings of unquoted shares, if the tax on them and other assets for which payment by instalments is permissible exceeds 20 per cent of the tax payable by one person in the same capacity.

If tax is payable by the recipient of a gift of the above types of assets (or by his estate if he has died before the relevant date) because the giver survived the recipient by less than seven years, the option to pay by instalments can also be claimed, but only if the assets are still owned by the recipient at the date of the giver's death or were still owned by the recipient at the date of the recipient's earlier death. If they are unquoted securities they must also have remained unquoted throughout the entire period between the original transfer and the giver's death.

When the asset is sold, or in the case of a trust asset it ceases to be held on trust, the instalment option ends and any unpaid tax becomes immediately payable.

Interest at a daily rate is charged on unpaid inheritance tax from the date it becomes due. In the cases of buildings, land which does not qualify for agricultural relief and shares in an investment or property company, interest is charged on the full amount of tax outstanding, but in the cases of the other assets which have the benefit of the instalment option interest is only charged if the instalment is overdue. The present rate of interest is 3 per cent per annum.

Any inheritance tax payable and not payable by later instalments, must be paid before the grant will be given to the personal representative. The Registry's fee and the amount of inheritance tax, if any, depend upon the value of the estate involved.

If the personal representatives do not have sufficient, or indeed any, money to pay the inheritance tax and the Registry's fee, but the estate includes National Savings Certificates, or SAYE contracts, or government stock on the Bank of England Register, or capital, deposit, children's, bonus, first option, pensioners guaranteed income, premium savings, or income bonds, the Registry can arrange for these assets to be used towards payment of the tax and fees and the applicants should request this at interview with the Registry.

Similarly, if the deceased had certificates of tax deposits, i.e. money on deposit with the Inland Revenue to meet future tax liabilities, that money can be used to pay inheritance tax before the grant of representation is issued.

If the deceased had money on deposit with a building society or bank, the building society or bank will usually allow as much of that money as is necessary to be used before probate for payment of inheritance tax. The system is voluntary but as yet not all banks have joined the scheme.

Sometimes stockbrokers will arrange for securities held by the deceased in their nominee accounts to be used to pay inheritance tax and probate fees, but this is not possible if the securities are held in certificated form and not in the broker's nominee account.

Payment of inheritance tax by using investments or deposits specified in the previous four paragraphs is made by completing and sending inheritance tax form D20 to the relevant institution which then makes the tax payment.

If there is no money or insufficient money on deposit to pay the tax, a building society or bank will usually be prepared to lend the necessary funds at interest for that purpose, and such interest is of course borne by the deceased's estate and not by the applicants for the grant personally. If possible the borrowing should be made by way of loan and not overdraft so that the interest is tax deductible. Interest on the loan should kept separately identifiable from interest on a loan obtained for any other purpose so that the interest on the loan for probate fees and/or inheritance tax can be deducted for income tax purposes from interest earned in the first year of winding up the estate.

When the inheritance tax has been paid, the Capital Taxes Office informs the Probate Registry, and the Probate Registry will send the grant of representation to the applicant by post. This does not necessarily mean that the Capital Taxes Office has finally agreed that the figures entered on the forms and the basis on which the tax is calculated are correct. The Capital Taxes Office might write with further questions and demanding further tax, and because the personal representative is primarily responsible for payment of tax, it is wise to write to the office asking for a formal clearance certificate from inheritance tax before finally passing the estate's money to those entitled. Formal clearance is obtained by sending to the Capital Taxes Office Form IHT 30 in duplicate, one copy of which the Revenue will return signed on behalf of the Revenue if it is satisfied that all the tax which is payable has been paid. The form can be obtained by post or downloaded from the Capital Taxes Office website.

THE PERSONAL REPRESENTATIVE'S POWER TO APPOINT AGENTS

When the Probate Registry has issued the grant of representation, the personal representative is fully empowered to administer the estate and wind up the financial matters and generally speaking he should do so personally. A personal representative is a trustee and he is bound by the various detailed and complex Acts of Parliament which regulate trustees' powers to delegate their responsibilities. His powers to appoint agents and delegate his functions are limited both as to whom he can appoint, for how long they can be appointed and as to the purpose for which they can be appointed.

An agent appointed by a personal representative cannot:

♦ further delegate powers delegated to him;

♦ appoint nominees, or custodians;

♦ appoint additional or new trustees of the estate;

♦ take a decision concerning the distribution of the assets of the estate;

♦ decide whether fees shall be paid out of income or capital.

A personal representative who appoints an agent to manage investments for the estate must agree with the agent in writing the investment policy to be followed.

If the personal representative expects to be unable to act personally over a long period and that he will need to appoint an agent to act for him, advice should be sought from a probate or trust solicitor. It might be simpler to consider appointing the proposed agent as attorney to take out the grant of representation in the first place so that the duration of his agency will not expire.

REGISTERING THE GRANT

What registration involves – in general

Registering the grant means producing it to the organisations, e.g. banks, with which the deceased had assets as proof of the personal representative's right to deal with the relevant asset.

At the interview with the Probate Registry the applicants will have been asked how many official copies (called office copies) of the grant were required and the copies will have been sent to the applicants with the original grant. An office copy bears the impression of the Registry's seal and is as good evidence of the right to deal with the assets of the estate as is the original grant. When dealing with the title to land it is sometimes necessary to endorse a record of the dealing on the original grant of representation and produce it later to show that the endorsement was made. Moreover an original grant of representation by virtue of its nature cannot be replaced. For these reasons when registering representation, and for fear of the original grant being lost in transit, it is usual to register an office copy of the grant rather than the original grant.

Sometimes it is necessary to send passbooks or share certificates when sending an office copy grant for registration and it is suggested that reference be made to the specimen letters which are to be found in Appendix 1. Quoting the passbook or share certificate account numbers in the letters and keeping a copy of the letters will possibly assist if the original documents be lost in transit.

Shares, debentures and loan stock

An official copy of the grant should be sent to the company's registrar with the relevant certificates as soon as possible, so that the registrar will be aware that future interest and dividend cheques should be made payable to the personal representatives and not to the deceased and to facilitate any subsequent sale or transfer of the shares or stock.

If it is intended to transfer the shares or loan stock to one or more beneficiaries, a completed transfer deed should be sent to the company's registrar with the relevant share or loan stock certificate and office copy of the grant. Transfer deeds can be obtained from law stationers or from the company's registrar and are simplicity itself to complete, but it should be noted that there is a section to be completed on the back of the deed.

The address of the relevant company's registrar can be obtained from the tax voucher which is sent with dividend or interest payments, from the company's website on the Internet or from the company's annual report. The address is also usually printed on share certificates, but one should be aware that companies do change their registrars from time to time and the registrar named on the share certificate might not be the current one, especially if the security has been held for some time.

If the securities are held in a stockbroker's nominee account instead of being certificated securities the grant of representation should be registered with the stockbrokers instead of registration with the Company's Registrar.

Dividend or interest cheques

If dividend or interest cheques payable to the deceased have been received since the death took place, it will be necessary to send an office copy of the grant to the drawer of the cheque with a request that a replacement cheque be issued or the old cheque be amended into the name of the personal representative and the amendment initialled by the drawer.

Insurance monies and pension arrears

The companies involved will have been written to when they were notified of the death and asked to state their requirements to enable payment to be made and these should now be complied with.

If the policy cannot be found the company will pay out upon an indemnity being given and a statutory declaration being made as to the circumstances. Usually the companies will prepare and supply these documents.

When requesting payment of the sum due, ask for interest from the date of death to the date of payment and how the total sum payable is split between the policy monies and interest, so that the amount attributable to tax will be known when it becomes necessary to complete the tax return for the administration period.

Debts owed to the estate

If the deceased was owed money when he died or money became due to him as a result of the death or payable to him since death, an office copy of the grant should be sent to the debtor with a request that payment be made to the executors.

Property which is security for a mortgage or any other liability

Instructions should not be given for the transfer, sale or other realisation of any such property unless the personal representative is absolutely certain that the estate is solvent, i.e. that there will be sufficient assets to cover payment of inheritance tax, the funeral and other expenses, debts and liabilities, because if this is not the case the creditor has a right to take and sell the property and prove in bankruptcy for any balance of his claim. If the sale produces more than is owed the creditor must account to the estate for the amount by which the net proceeds of the sale exceed the debt.

8

Paying Off the Debts and Discharging the Liabilities of the Estate

If assets need to be realised to provide money for payment of the estate's debts and administration expenses, consult closely with the beneficiaries as to which are to be sold and which are to be retained for final distribution to the beneficiaries, so that their wishes are complied with as far as the law allows.

ADVERTISEMENTS FOR CREDITORS AND CLAIMANTS
Before distributing the assets of the estate among the beneficiaries, a personal representative who has not already done so should consider publishing the statutory advertisement for claimants and creditors referred to under 'Debts and liabilities' on pp. 92 and 93 for the reason given there.

WHAT DEBTS AND LIABILITIES MUST BE PAID?
Most debts, contracts and liabilities of a person survive death and must be paid or fulfilled by the personal representative. An exception is that contracts to the performance of which the personality of the deceased is essential, e.g. of a musician to perform at a concert or an author to write a book, do not survive death. The personal representative has a right to be reimbursed, out of the assets of the estate, for the payments he makes and the liabilities he incurs in the performance of his

duties. He has no right to claim payment for work done in respect of the estate unless the will authorises payment.

TO WHOM SHOULD PAYMENT BE MADE?

Bankrupts

Payment should not be made to a beneficiary or to a creditor who is bankrupt; the entitlement is that of the trustee in bankruptcy. To discover whether a person is or is not bankrupt a search should be made against that person's name in the Alphabetical Index of Names at the Land Charges Registry. The current fee for such a search is £1 per name and search forms can be purchased from law stationers. In the event of difficulty a solicitor can be requested to make the search.

Persons of unsound mind

Similarly, if a debt is owing to a person who is not believed to be of sound mind, the debt should not be paid to that person personally but to his receiver or to his attorney appointed under an enduring power of attorney made before the creditor lost his sanity.

Future debts

If the personal representative knows of debts or liabilities of the estate which might arise in the future, then before distributing the estate, he should protect himself and make provision for settling them. He can do this by:

1. obtaining an indemnity from the beneficiary against the claims; or

2. retaining a sufficient sum from the property in respect of which the liability may arise, or if the liability is not

contingent in respect of any particular asset of the estate, from the general estate; or

3. asking a court to direct him as to what should be done to cover the liability.

The risk with course 1 is that an indemnity is only as good financially as the person who gives it. The problem with course 2 is quantifying the extent of the liability and obtaining the beneficiary's agreement to that sum, and the problem with course 3 is the expense to the estate of the court application.

INCOME AND CAPITAL GAINS TAX

Remember before distributing the estate that the final position in respect of income and capital gains taxes (including tax on income received since death and prior to final distribution of the estate, and capital gains made upon the sale of assets during that period) must be established by completing income tax returns for the administration period and any outstanding tax paid. This is dealt with in detail on pages 90 to 91 and 143 to 147.

FINALISING INHERITANCE TAX

If inheritance tax has been paid on stock exchange securities (other than those quoted on the AIM market), shares in common investment funds, unit trusts and land or buildings which are sold in the course of administration of the estate at a loss compared with their value as declared in the probate papers, it might be worth reconsidering the value attributed to them for inheritance tax purposes with a view to obtaining a partial refund of the tax.

Before deciding to elect for an Inheritance Tax revaluation, bear in mind that if assets are re-valued for Inheritance Tax purposes to reflect a fall in value between the date of death and the date they are disposed of by transfer to the beneficiary or sale, the reduced value becomes the base cost (i.e. the value at which the assets are deemed to have been acquired), for the transferee for Capital Gains Tax purposes and check the Inheritance Tax Rates and the Capital Gains Tax rates at the relevant date.

To obtain agreement by the Revenue to a revaluation in the case of stock exchange securities, shares in common investment funds and unit trusts, the personal representatives must have sold them within 12 months of the date of the death. To recalculate the amount of tax properly payable, the loss is deducted from the declared value of the estate and is calculated by deducting the *gross* proceeds of sale from the value declared for probate purposes. No allowance is made for the expenses of sale and all the quoted investments in the estate must be taken into account, not merely those sold at a loss. If the personal representatives reinvest the proceeds of sale by buying further unit trusts, common investment funds or quoted investments within two months of the last sale during the 12-month period, the amount of repayable tax will be restricted.

Similar principles apply in the case of land or buildings, the differences being that the period for the sale is four years instead of 12 months, the period for reinvestment is four months after the last qualifying sale in the period of three years from death instead of two months during the period of 12 months from death, and sales at a profit in the fourth year after death or which result in a profit or loss of less than 5 per cent or £1,000 are ignored.

INSOLVENT ESTATES

In cases in which the assets of the estate are sufficient to pay all the funeral and testamentary expenses and the debts and liabilities of the deceased, there is no problem as to which should be paid, but if the estate is insolvent i.e. the assets are insufficient to pay them all, there is a complicated special order in which they must be discharged. It is as well to consult a solicitor if the estate is insolvent because a personal representative who wrongly pays a creditor before another who has precedence, incurs personal liability to the wronged creditor.

9

Distributing the Remaining Assets

PRECAUTIONS TO TAKE BEFORE MAKING DISTRIBUTIONS FROM THE ESTATE FUNDS

Advertisements for creditors and claimants

Before distributing the assets of the estate amongst the beneficiaries, a personal representative who has not already done so should consider publishing the statutory advertisement for claimants and creditors referred to in the previous chapter and under 'Debts and liabilities' on page 92. for the reason given there.

Check identities and relationships

A personal representative who distributes assets or an incorrect sum might well be held personally responsible and unable to recover from the recipient. It is wise therefore to draw up a family tree supported by birth, marriage and death certificates where appropriate, rather than to rely upon hearsay to the effect that A and B were legally married or registered a Civil Partnership or that C died many years ago. If the sums are substantial and a point is not entirely clear, consider employing a professional genealogist. Unless the people involved are personally well known to the personal representative he always should ask for evidence of identity when distributing the estate.

Obtain an Inheritance Tax clearance certificate

It is wise to write to the Capital Taxes Office and request a formal inheritance tax clearance certificate, i.e. formal confirmation that no claim will be made by the Revenue for further inheritance tax, before distributing any assets to beneficiaries. A clearance certificate will protect the personal representative against future claims for inheritance tax in relation to the estate and give him the confidence of knowing that all the valuations have been accepted by the Revenue for inheritance tax purposes.

THE POSSIBILITY OF CLAIMS UNDER THE INHERITANCE (PROVISION FOR FAMILY AND DEPENDANTS) ACT 1975 AS AMENDED

The personal representative should also wait for six months from the date of the grant of representation being issued by the Registry before distributing any assets to beneficiaries because of the possibility of claims being made against the estate under the Inheritance (Provision for Family and Dependants) Act 1975 as amended. If a claim is made immediate assistance should be sought from a solicitor.

In broad terms the act permits claims to a reasonable share of the estate after death, even if the will leaves the claimant nothing. Claimants could be:

◆ a wife, husband or registered civil partner;

◆ a former wife, former husband or former registered civil partner who has not remarried or entered into a new civil partnership;

◆ children (adopted children claim against the estates of their adoptive parents, not the estates of their birth parents);

- any person who was treated as a child of any marriage or civil partnership to which the deceased has been a party;

- anyone who considers that he or she was maintained by the deceased to a material extent immediately before death.

Maintenance need not be for any minimum period or financial; it can be maintenance provided in kind e.g. by providing free food and lodgings.

A successful spouse or registered civil partner will be awarded what is reasonable whether or not it is required for the claimant's maintenance; any other claimant will only receive maintenance.

What is reasonable depends upon all the circumstances of the case. The High Court put it rather well when it quoted with approval a Canadian court which ruled that reasonable maintenance was enough to enable the applicant (a child of the deceased who was an able bodied adult) to live 'neither luxuriously, nor miserably but decently and comfortably'. Matters which are likely to be considered include the size of the estate, the behaviour of the parties and of the deceased, the length of time that the relationship existed, and the resources and needs (including those arising from mental or physical disabilities) of the parties. In assessing a claimant's financial situation a court can hold it against a claimant that he has in the past invested in speculative investments or lived beyond his means.

A partner who was cohabiting with the deceased in the same household as if they were man and wife or civil partners for two years immediately prior to the death can claim without having to prove that he or she was maintained by the deceased.

What is meant by the word 'immediately' has to be construed in the light of all the surrounding circumstances and can have a wider meaning than might at first be thought. The case of Gully v Dix in re Dix deceased, which was decided by the Court of Appeal in January 2004, is a good example. The facts were that the claimant and the deceased lived together from 1974 until August 2001 when the claimant moved out because the deceased's alcoholism caused her to fear for her safety (he threatened to kill her). In October 2001 the deceased died. Even though she had not returned before the death, as far as the claimant was concerned, the relationship was not over and the three months separation was unusual rather than the 'settled situation'. The court decided that the important word was 'household' not 'house'. To decide whether the claimant was being maintained by the deceased and whether she and the deceased were living together in the same household immediately before the death, it was necessary to look at the reason for her leaving and the entire period during which they had been living together, not just the last three months. In the light of their long standing relationship, in spite of the fact that she had been away from the house for the three months or so before the death, the court decided that the claimant could be considered to be living in the same household as the deceased immediately before his death and was therefore entitled to make a claim.

The High Court or a County Court exercising matrimonial jurisdiction can bar a spouse or civil partner from making a claim under the Act on or after successful proceedings for annulment of marriage, divorce, judicial separation or dissolution of civil partnership.

It should also be noted that section 9 (1) of the Act provides that if 'a deceased person was immediately before his death beneficially entitled to a joint tenancy of any property . . . the court . . . may order that the deceased's severable share of that property . . . be treated . . . as part of the net estate of the deceased'.

Proceedings under the Act can be brought in the County Court or in The High Court, but they must be started within six months of the issue of a grant of representation to the estate unless the claimant can satisfy the court that there were exceptional reasons for the delay.

VARYING THE TERMS OF A WILL OR THE INHERITANCE RULES OF INTESTACY AFTER DEATH

It is common knowledge that a person can vary the provisions of a will during his lifetime, but it is not so well known that the provisions of a valid will or the normal laws of inheritance applicable on intestacy are sometimes, quite legally, changed by the beneficiaries after someone's death. Also if a beneficiary of an estate inherits by surviving his benefactor's death and then dies, his personal representatives can disclaim or vary his inheritance if they have the consent of those who benefit under his will or intestacy.

Types of variation

The changes may take place either:

◆ with the consent of all the beneficiaries affected (usually set out in a deed known as a deed of family arrangement, although the document need not be a deed and any form of writing will be sufficient); or

◆ with the consent of one or more beneficiaries (as when a surviving spouse or civil partner decides to exercise the right given to her by the law in the case of an intestacy to take a capital sum instead of income during the remainder of her life, or a beneficiary under a will disclaims the inheritance); or

◆ without the consent of the beneficiaries as a result of, say, a successful claim under the Inheritance (Provision for Family and Dependants) Act 1975 as amended.

Reasons to vary

The reasons for wishing to change the terms of a will are many and various, for example:

◆ Sometimes a will has not been updated for many years and the circumstances in which it was made may have completely changed by the date of death.

◆ Sometimes it is decided to settle claims made under the Inheritance (Provision for Family and Dependants) Act 1975 as amended by entering into an out-of-court settlement.

◆ Instead of settling the question by an expensive application to a court, executors and beneficiaries might wish to settle problems created by poor drafting or typing of the will by agreement and to record the agreement in writing rather than risk further disputes.

◆ It might be desired to give executors wider powers than are provided for in the will, e.g. to widen the executors' powers in relation to the investment of bequests made to underage beneficiaries.

◆ The beneficiaries might wish to provide for someone considered to have been overlooked or wealthy people might wish to substitute bequests to their children or grandchildren for bequests to themselves.

◆ The most common reason of all is to alter the provisions of the will in such a way as to ensure that less tax is incurred, although alterations purely for the purpose of saving tax are open to challenge by the Inland Revenue.

The difference between a variation and a disclaimer

Some changes to the provisions of a will or to the devolution of an estate under the laws of intestacy can save very considerable amounts of tax if the estate is large, but others increase the amount of tax payable. The changes can affect not only inheritance tax, but also capital gains tax, income tax and means tested Social Security benefit payments, and may cost substantial sums in Stamp Duty and legal fees to implement, but in the right circumstances and if carefully and knowledgeably done, they can be very worthwhile. It is essential that advice should be taken from a solicitor or accountant who is knowledgeable about tax law before such a course of action is finally embarked upon. Suffice it to say here that if a change is to be made, the difference between disclaiming something to be inherited from a will or under the laws of intestacy and varying the provisions of a will or the laws of intestacy must be clearly understood.

To disclaim a benefit under a will or an entitlement under an intestacy is to refuse to accept it and although a disclaimer can be retracted, it can only be retracted if no other person has relied upon it to their detriment. A disclaimer can only be made if the person seeking to disclaim has not already benefited from the inheritance which it is sought to disclaim. The inherited benefit cannot be accepted as to part and refused as to part; it is all or nothing, although if more than one gift is made to the same beneficiary in a will or inherited on intestacy, one gift may be accepted and the other or others may be refused and disclaimed, provided they are clearly separate gifts.

On the other hand, to effect a variation one first accepts the gift and then varies it so that another or others benefit, either in addition to or to the exclusion of oneself. This point is very important because it necessarily follows that having accepted the inheritance in the case of a variation, one can decide its further devolution and decide who is to benefit from it, but having refused the inheritance in the case of a disclaimer one has no further control over it, and it must devolve according to the other provisions of the will or the laws of intestacy or otherwise, as the case may be. It should be noted that it necessarily follows that although it is possible to effect a variation of the devolution of jointly owned property which is inherited as the result of being a surviving joint tenant, it is not possible to disclaim survivorship rights.

It follows that different inheritance, capital gains and income tax consequences result from the difference in the nature of a disclaimer and a variation, and as stated above, before making a decision, it is essential that specialist tax advice be sought.

Conditions for tax-effective variations and disclaimers
If the Revenue is to consider the change as having been made by the deceased and there is to be a saving of inheritance and/or capital gains tax, the following conditions must be complied with:

◆ The change must be made in writing and in the case of a variation all the parties affected must be parties to the document to show they consent to the changes. However, in the case of a disclaimer, only the person making the disclaimer is a party to the document.

◆ The disclaimer or variation must be made within two years of the death.

◆ The document which makes a variation must contain a statement which must be made by all parties to it to the effect that it is to have effect for the purposes of Inheritance Tax and /or Capital Gains Tax.

If the variation results in more tax becoming payable, the Personal Representatives must be parties to the document unless, in that capacity, they hold no or insufficient funds to pay the additional tax. If additional tax is payable a fine can be imposed upon all parties to the document unless a copy of the document and a note of the additional tax payable is supplied to the Revenue within six months of the date of the document.

There is no necessity for a disclaimer to state that it is intended to take effect from the date of death; it does so automatically.

To consent to the change a party must be of full age and have full legal capacity. If this is a problem, for example if a person is under the age of 18, or not of sound mind or if a benefit which it is desired to change has been given to a person who has not yet been born, a court can be asked to consent on that person's behalf, but a court will only give consent if it considers that the transaction is for that person's benefit. Moreover, an application to a court is expensive. The fact that court proceedings are not quick can also make it difficult to comply with the time limit which will not usually be extended.

It is not possible to disclaim an inheritance which is expected from the estate of someone who has not yet died.

Suffice it to repeat that these matters are not for a layman, and if it is thought that circumstances exist in which they might be of assistance, prompt professional assistance should be sought.

INTEREST ON LEGACIES
It is necessary to differentiate between specific legacies i.e. legacies of specific things e.g. 'the balance standing to the credit of my account with Barclays Bank Plc' and general legacies e.g. 'the sum of one hundred pounds'. The legatee of a specific legacy is entitled to the income it produces from the date of death. Unless the will states to the contrary, interest is payable on general legacies at 4 per cent per annum from the date from which they are properly payable, and in the absence of any specific provision in the will that is one year from the date of death even if the will states that they are to be paid as soon as possible. Interest on a general legacy is treated as gross income in the hands of the beneficiary who must pay tax on it. The interest can be deducted when calculating the income of the estate during the administration period for income tax purposes. Legacies can be paid earlier than one year from the date of death, if convenient, but should not be paid less than six months from the date of the issue of the grant of representation in case a successful claim is made under the Inheritance (Provision for Family and Dependants) Act 1975 as amended.

INTERPRETING A WILL AND DECIDING WHAT BEQUESTS AND LIABILITIES SHOULD BE FULFILLED

Is the document a valid will?

The first thing to do when considering a will is to make sure that it is the last legally effective will. This subject has been dealt with in Chapter 6, pages 57 to 64.

What does the will mean and are the bequests legally effective?

Wills that deal with foreign property

When considering the provisions of a will in respect of any property the testator may have which is situated abroad, it is necessary to consider the foreign law relating to the property and the making of wills, even if the will is made in the United Kingdom. Some countries have restrictions in relation to who can inherit property and the tax laws relating to property differ from those of English law. The procedure and formalities for making a will that is to be recognised by the foreign country as a valid document of title to the property are also usually different from those of England and Wales.

When dealing with wills which have a foreign element it is essential to seek the assistance of a lawyer qualified to practise in the foreign country. The Law Society or the relevant foreign embassy will be able to supply contact details of a suitable lawyer.

Section 41 of the Inheritance Tax Act 1984

When distributing the assets of an estate and dealing with a bequest which under the law would be exempt from inheritance tax, it is necessary to bear in mind this statutory provision which will apply whatever the will might say to the contrary.

The relevant bequests which under the law are exempt from inheritance tax are:

♦ gifts of any amount to a spouse or civil partner, unless the testator is domiciled in the United Kingdom but the spouse or partner is not, in which case the exemption is limited to £55,000.

♦ gifts to registered charities for charitable purposes.

♦ gifts for certain national purposes including gifts to most museums and art galleries and to political parties which have at least 2 sitting members of the House of Commons or which have 1 sitting member and whose candidates polled 150,000 votes at the last general election.

♦ gifts of land to registered Housing Associations.

In essence the Section means that such a bequest shall not be made to bear, either directly or indirectly, any of the inheritance tax payable on the death. If a will gives the testator's estate to his executors or trustees, for example, 'upon trust to use it to pay my funeral and testamentary expenses, debts and inheritance tax payable in respect of my estate and to divide what remains equally between such of my wife and my son as shall survive me and if both then equally between them', the executors must first pay the funeral and testamentary expenses and debts, secondly notionally divide what remains equally between the surviving wife and son and thirdly pay all the inheritance tax out of the son's notional share before distributing what remains of the son's share to him and the widow's share to her. To pay the inheritance tax, as the will directs should be done, before making the notional division between the widow and the son, would be in breach of Section 41 in that it would be indirectly making the widow's share (which is by statute exempt from inheritance tax), bear tax.

Uncertainty, ambiguity and the court's power to rectify a will to carry out the testator's intention
If a court is satisfied that a will does not carry out the testator's intention because of a clerical error or the failure of the person who prepared the will to understand the testator's intentions, the court can rectify the will so as to carry out the testator's intentions e.g. if a clause has been omitted by mistake. However, courts have very limited powers to look beyond the wording of a will to ascertain the testator's intention. They are only permitted to do so if the wording of the will is meaningless or if it is shown to be ambiguous on the face of the will or in the light of surrounding circumstances. If this is not so and the wording of the will appears to show the testator's intentions clearly, the courts have no power to hear evidence as to what was actually intended and must give effect to the testator's wishes *as expressed* in the will, even though external evidence would have shown that the wording of the will did not express those wishes correctly.

If the intention in any part of the will is still not clear after taking into account any external evidence which it is permissible to consider, a court and the executors must ignore that part of the will and it will not take effect.

Bequests which fail to take effect

The effect of divorce or annulment of marriage or annulment of civil partnership
Dissolution of marriage or civil partnership does not invalidate a Will, but a decree absolute (not a decree nisi),

makes any bequest in the will to the spouse or civil partner take effect as if the former spouse or partner had died on the date the decree becomes absolute, leaving bequests in the remainder of the will valid. Usually the bequest will become part of the residue of the estate and go to the residuary beneficiaries, but if the bequest is of the entire estate or of a share of the residue of the estate, it will be treated as not having been disposed of by the will and will be inherited according to the laws of intestacy.

Similarly, the provisions in a will conferring powers of appointment on a spouse or partner (i.e. power for him to appoint or choose a beneficiary for part of an estate) or appointing him as an executor or trustee, take effect after a decree of dissolution of marriage or civil partnership as if the former spouse or civil partner had died on the date the decree became absolute.

Unless a contrary intention is apparent from the will, an appointment of a spouse or civil partner as a guardian of an underage child is revoked by a decree absolute, annulment or dissolution which is either made in a court in England or Wales or would be recognised by such a court.

Bequests to the witness to a will or witness's spouse
or civil partner
Two independent witnesses to the testator's signature to a will are required to make a will or codicil valid, and if a beneficiary or the beneficiary's spouse or civil partner witnesses the will or codicil, the intended beneficiary will lose the bequest made by the document unless the offending witness's signature can be regarded as superfluous because there are two other disinterested witnesses.

If there are not two other disinterested witnesses, although the person who is named in a will as the beneficiary will lose the bequest, the remainder of the will will not be affected.

Bequests contrary to public policy
Conditions attached to gifts and gifts themselves may be void and of no effect because they are contrary to the public policy of the moment. Exactly what is considered to be contrary to public policy changes from time to time and if there is any doubt advice from a lawyer should be sought. A few general principles can be stated.

Conditions that weaken the family unit or the institution of marriage are contrary to public policy, as are conditions that interfere with the choice of one's religion. Therefore a condition attached to a gift to a son that it is dependent upon the son leaving his wife or converting to Catholicism will not take effect because both conditions are void being contrary to public policy.

Conditions contrary to the inherent legal nature of property, e.g. that it shall not be sold or shall be boarded up and not used for a long specified time, are contrary to public policy.

A provision in a will that a bequest is to be forfeited if the beneficiary challenges the will is not considered to be contrary to public policy, but the bequest might fail to take effect for reasons of uncertainty, unless it is carefully drafted.

If the condition upon which the bequest is given is merely prohibited by law or public policy, the condition will be void, but if the bequest is considered to be essentially evil, e.g. a bequest conditional upon murdering someone, the bequest will fail completely.

If the intention is that the gift shall only take effect if the condition is fulfilled (i.e. the condition is what is known as a condition precedent) and the condition is void, the gift will fail completely, but if the intention is that the gift shall take effect but cease if the condition is fulfilled, i.e. the condition is what is known as a condition subsequent, the gift takes effect free from the void condition. An example of a gift with a condition precedent is a gift to a son if he successfully completes the university course he is taking, and an example of a condition subsequent is a gift to him, but if he fails the course, then to the testator's daughter, although both of these conditions are of course valid ones.

Gifts which break the rules against perpetuities and accumulations
The law contains very complex rules which prevent the income from a bequest being accumulated and added to the capital of the bequest by the personal representatives for an excessive period, rather than distributed to the beneficiary, and which prevent bequests being made to beneficiaries whose identity might not be ascertained for an excessively long time in the future. These rules are known as the rules against perpetuities and accumulations and are mainly contained in The Perpetuity and Accumulations Act 1964. If a bequest has been made and the identity of the beneficiary might not be ascertained within twenty-one years of the testator's death, e.g. a gift 'to my grandchildren whether born before or after my death', be sure to consult a solicitor about the wording and its legal effect. Similarly if the income from a bequest is to be accumulated for a period which could exceed twenty-one years, consult a solicitor.

If in doubt, take legal advice.

Irreconcilable bequests
Generally speaking, if two clauses of a will are clearly irreconcilable, effect should be given to the later clause and not to the former, but again, if there is the slightest doubt, take legal advice.

Insufficient assets
If there are insufficient assets to pay all the debts and liabilities there is a specific, complex order in which the debts must be paid and it is essential to seek legal advice.

Properly payable debts, liabilities of the estate and funeral and testamentary expenses are payable in priority to bequests made by the will or claims to entitlement by the next of kin.

When there is sufficient money to pay all the funeral and testamentary expenses and the debts and liabilities of the deceased, but insufficient to pay all the beneficiaries named in the will, then unless there is any contrary provision in the will, those who are bequeathed specific things should have their bequests first, followed by those who are bequeathed specific amounts of money. If there is not enough to pay all the gifts of money they are reduced in proportion.

Bequests to people who have predeceased the testator or organisations which have ceased to exist
Unless there is a provision to the contrary in the will or the gift is made to fulfil a moral or legal obligation (e.g. to repay a debt which has been discharged under the law of bankruptcy or which is statute barred), a gift made by will to a person who died before the testator or to an organisation which no longer exists at the time of the testator's death fails and does not take effect. An exception to this general rule is contained in Section 33 of the Wills Act 1837 (as amended). By this

section a bequest to a descendant of the testator who dies before the testator, leaving a descendant who is living at the testator's death, will take effect as a bequest to the descendant who is living at the testator's death, unless the will shows a contrary intention.

Bequests of items which no longer exist
If the testator no longer has such an article as is described in a gift (e.g. my gold watch where the watch has been sold or lost after the making of the will), the gift does not take effect, but if the testator, having had such an article, disposes of it and acquires another fitting the description (i.e. another gold watch), the gift takes effect in respect of the substituted object (the new gold watch). In other words, unless there is evidence that the contrary is intended as regards things given by will, the will takes effect in the circumstances which exist at the moment of death. However, this rule does not apply to the description of persons in whose favour gifts are made by will, e.g. a gift to 'John's wife', the rule being that the bequest is to the person who fulfilled the description at the time that the will was made and only if there is no such person does the person who fulfils the description at the time of death or later inherit.

Gifts of other people's property
There is a rule in English law known as the doctrine of election to the effect that a person who accepts a benefit conferred by a document must also accept every other provision of that document and give up any other right he possesses which is inconsistent with the document. Thus if a testator who does not own an asset purports to give it away by his will and also gives a gift to the true owner of the asset, the true owner must either refuse his bequest or give up his own property or the value in compensation to the other beneficiary.

Perhaps an example will make the point clearer. If Farmer George dies and leaves 'my farm Blackacre to my son William and my London flat to my brother Jack' but in fact he does not own Blackacre which belongs to Jack, Jack must decide whether he will take the flat and give up Blackacre or its value to William or decline the bequest of the flat.

Legacies to creditors

Unless an intention to the contrary is shown, there is a presumption that a legacy to a creditor which is equal to or greater than the debt owed is given in satisfaction and payment of the debt. An intention may be shown to the contrary if, for example, the will directs the executor to pay all the testator's debts or if the legacy is payable only at a future date or upon the happening of an event in the future.

Substitutional legacies

In the absence of evidence to the contrary, if a will bequeaths the same thing or an identical sum, twice, to the same legatee, the legatee is only entitled to one of the legacies and it is assumed that the second legacy is a repetition of the first. If the two legacies are of unequal amounts or are given in different documents, e.g. one in a will and the other in a codicil to the will, the presumption does not apply and both are payable.

Bequest to a spouse or civil partner followed by the same bequest to issue

If a will or codicil leaves an absolute gift to the testator's spouse or civil partner but the same document purports to give an interest in the same property to his issue, then, unless the document shows a contrary intention, the spouse or partner will inherit the property absolutely, and the purported gift to the issue will not take effect.

The meaning of certain words.
In construing words used in a will or codicil to decide what they mean the words must be considered in the context in which they are used and the document must be considered as a whole. Therefore the same word may have a different meaning in a different document.

'Personal estate', 'my personal effects', 'my goods and chattels' and 'my belongings'
These words are usually taken to include all moveable items, but not freehold or leasehold property but 'my estate' or 'my possessions' is usually construed as meaning all the testator's assets including non-moveable property.

'Personal' estate or 'Personal' chattels should not usually be construed to include items used for business purposes. A useful and comprehensive, if somewhat dated, definition of personal chattels can be found in section 55 (1) (x) of the Administration of Estates Act 1925:

> 'Personal chattels' mean carriages, horses, stable furniture and effects (not used for business purposes), motor cars and accessories (not used for business purposes), garden effects, domestic animals, plate, plated articles, linen, china, glass, books, pictures, prints, furniture, jewellery, articles of household or personal use or ornament, musical and scientific instruments and apparatus, wines, liquors and consumable stores, but do not include any chattels used at the death . . . for business purposes nor money or securities for money.

'Survive me'
An interesting example of the rule that the meaning of words in a will must be gleaned from the context in which they are

used is to be found in the case of Blech v Blech which showed that a reference to a beneficiary surviving the testatrix did not necessarily imply that the beneficiary must be living at the date of the death of the testatrix. B created a trust for the children of her son R who survived her and attained the age of 21 years and if more than one for them in equal shares. The court decided that, bearing in mind that it would be 17 years before the oldest of those children of R who were living at the date of B's will reached the age of 21, B must have thought that R might have more children during that period. Consequently it decided that B intended that two children who were born to R after B's death and reached the stated age must be considered to have 'survived' her and should be allowed to share with the qualifying children born before her death.

'Month'
'Month' means calendar month unless lunar month or four weeks is specifically stated.

'From'
'From' a date does not include the date.

'Children'
The word 'children' in a will or codicil means children and does not include grandchildren or stepchildren, unless the will shows a contrary intention or unless the context or circumstances so require, for example if the testator had no children living at the date the will was made.

The law in relation to wills and devolution of estates on intestacy makes no distinction between adopted, legitimate and illegitimate children and a reference to children is taken to include them all, unless there is an indication to the contrary.

'Issue' and 'descendants'
A gift to 'issue' or 'descendants' means that each of such
people who are living at the date of death inherit an equal
share unless the gift is stated to be to the issue or to the
descendants 'per stirpes'. If the gift is stated to be given per
stirpes only the first generation of descendants inherit unless
one of them has died before the testator, in which case *his* next
generation of descendants inherit their deceased parent's share
equally between them.

'Relations' or 'next of kin'
The words 'relations' or 'next of kin' will usually be taken to
mean those who would inherit the estate if the deceased died
intestate. (Please refer to the next section of this chapter.)

DISTRIBUTION IN ACCORDANCE WITH THE LAWS
OF INTESTACY
If someone dies without making a will he is said to die
intestate and his estate is inherited according to intestacy law.
A few general points first:

Intestacy law divides relatives into groups or classes according
to their blood relationship to the deceased, e.g. children,
siblings, grandparents, etc. All members of a given class
inherit in equal shares. If a member of one class has died
before the deceased and leaves issue who survive the deceased,
the issue inherit the share which their predeceasing parent
would have inherited had he survived, equally between them.
There is a specific order in which the various classes inherit
and if all members of a given class have died before the
deceased without leaving issue who survived the deceased, the
next class inherits. The words 'child' and 'children' are used to
mean a person's immediate descendants (as opposed to
grandchildren) and do not include a stepchild or stepchildren,

but no distinction is made between legitimate and illegitimate children. Adopted children inherit from their adoptive parents and not from their natural parents.

The word 'issue' is used to include children and/or grandchildren. If those entitled to inherit are under the age of 18, the inheritance is held in trust for them until they either reach the age of 18, marry or enter into a registered civil partnership under that age. Net estate means the estate after deducting all debts, liabilities, inheritance tax and funeral and testamentary expenses.

To decide who is entitled to inherit, look for the first class and if there is no member of the class who survived the deceased or predeceased him leaving issue who survived him, move on to the next class.

The first person to have a claim on the estate is the surviving spouse or registered civil partner, and the amount to which he or she is entitled depends upon the size of the estate and whether or not there are any surviving issue or certain other close relatives. If the spouse or partner survived, but for a period of less than 28 days beginning on the day on which the intestate died, the spouse or partner is considered to have not survived the intestate.

- ◆ *If the deceased left a surviving spouse or registered civil partner but no issue and no parent, brother or sister of the whole blood or issue of a brother or sister of the whole blood,* the surviving spouse or partner inherits the entire estate.

- ◆ *If the deceased left a surviving spouse or civil partner and issue or any of the specified relatives,* the surviving spouse or partner is entitled to the deceased's personal chattels, i.e. moveable items such as sporting trophies or motor car, but

personal chattels does not include items used in any
business e.g. a delivery van.

The surviving spouse or civil partner is also entitled to a fixed
sum of money known as a statutory legacy and interest on the
statutory legacy until payment at the rate of 6 per cent from
the date of death.

If the deceased is survived by issue the spouse's or partner's
statutory legacy is £125,000. If there are no surviving issue but
there is a surviving parent, brother or sister of the whole blood
surviving, or issue of a brother or sister of the whole blood
who died before the deceased, the legacy is £200,000.

The surviving spouse or civil partner is further entitled to one
half of what is known as 'the residuary estate' i.e. what
remains of the net estate after deducting the personal chattels
and the statutory legacy. If there are surviving issue, the
surviving spouse or partner is entitled to the share of the
residuary estate only during his or her lifetime, but if there is
no surviving issue, then the surviving spouse or partner is
entitled to the share for his or her use and benefit absolutely.
Where the spouse or partner is only entitled to the half share
of the residuary estate during his or her remaining lifetime,
because it has to be left for those who are entitled to inherit it
after his or her own death, the spouse or partner can only
spend the income that share produces and cannot spend the
capital sum represented by the share. Where the spouse or
partner is entitled to the share for his or her own use and
benefit absolutely he or she can, of course, dispose of both the
capital and income as he or she wishes.

A surviving spouse or registered civil partner is entitled to
require the personal representative to use the residuary estate

to purchase his interest for life in the one half share of the residuary estate from him. To do so he must give notice of the requirement within 12 months to the administrators of the estate, or if he is the only administrator, to the Senior Registrar of the High Court. If the matrimonial home is freehold or leasehold with at least two years of the lease unexpired at the date of death, the spouse or partner can also insist, within a year of the issue of the grant of representation, upon using his share of the residuary estate to buy the matrimonial home, paying any difference in value in cash. The purchase price is the value of the home at the date of the acquisition, not the value at the date of death. In cases where the matrimonial home:

◆ is part of a building or agricultural estate contained in the residuary estate; or

◆ used in part or entirely as a hotel or lodging house; or

◆ in part for other than domestic purposes,

the right cannot be exercised unless a court is satisfied that it is not likely to diminish the value of the other assets in the residuary estate or make them more difficult to dispose of.

◆ *If the deceased left a surviving spouse or registered civil partner and issue*, the issue inherit one half of the residuary estate on the deceased's death and the other one half of the residuary estate after the death of the surviving spouse or civil partner as the case may be.

◆ *If the deceased left a surviving spouse or registered civil partner and no issue*, the one half share of the residuary estate not inherited by the surviving spouse or partner absolutely is inherited by the deceased's parent if one survives him, or if no parent has survived, by brothers or sisters of the whole blood and issue of deceased brothers and sisters of the whole blood, the issue of the deceased brothers or sisters inheriting equally between them the share which their deceased parent would have taken had he survived.

- *If the deceased left no surviving spouse or civil partner but left issue* the net estate is inherited by the issue.

- *If the deceased left no surviving spouse or civil partner and left no issue but left a parent or parents*, the net estate is inherited by the parent(s), and if both, then by them equally.

- *If the deceased left no spouse, civil partner, issue, or parent,* the net estate is inherited by the following classes of people living at the death and in the following order so that if there is no-one in a class living at the death the subsequent class inherit viz. brothers and sisters of the whole blood, or if none, brothers and sisters of the half blood or if none, grandparents or if none, uncles and aunts of the whole blood or if none by uncles and aunts of the half blood.

- *If the deceased was survived by none of the above* the Crown, the Duchy of Cornwall or Duchy of Lancaster inherits the estate.

A person is considered to be a spouse for the purposes of the laws of intestacy until a decree absolute (not a decree nisi) of divorce or a judicial separation (other than in the magistrates' court) has been pronounced, and to be a civil partner from when the partnership is registered until it is dissolved.

TO WHOM SHOULD DISTRIBUTIONS BE MADE?

Children conceived by artificial insemination or in vitro fertilisation

When distributing to those known to have been conceived by artificial insemination or by in vitro fertilisation the following rules should be kept in mind.

Except for inheritance of titles, and land which devolves with titles, if a child is artificially conceived (i.e. as a result of artificial insemination or in vitro fertilisation):

♦ in the case of a couple who are married and not judicially separated, the husband is considered to be the father unless it is proved that he did not consent to the conception;

♦ in the case of treatment provided for a man and woman together, the man is considered to be the father irrespective of whether or not his sperm was used;

♦ the mother is the woman who has carried the child as the result of the placing in her of an embryo or of an egg or sperm.

Although The Human Fertilisation and Embryology (Deceased Fathers) Act 2003 permits a deceased husband or partner to be registered as the father of a child conceived after his death by the use of his sperm, the registration does not give the child any rights of inheritance. (The reason for the rule is to avoid delay in the winding up of estates.)

Underage beneficiaries

Unless permitted to do so by the will, neither a person under the age of 18 nor that person's parent or guardian can give a valid receipt for the capital of a bequest (as opposed to the income it produces) and consequently neither can give a valid discharge for any capital payment made to him. A valid receipt for income produced by a bequest to a person who is under the age of 18 can only be given by the person, or his parent or guardian, if the beneficiary is married or in a registered civil partnership. Accordingly a personal representative should not make any capital payment to a minor, or any income payment to an unmarried minor who is not in a registered civil partnership, unless authorised by the will and should either retain the sum due in the personal representative's name on behalf of the underage beneficiary until the beneficiary becomes of age, or arrange for it to be paid into court.

If the bequest is retained in the personal representative's name, it should be invested in authorised investments and be designated as in respect of the beneficiary to avoid the possibility of the investments being confused with the personal investments of the personal representative.

Authorised investments are those authorised by the will or other document creating the trust and in addition those permitted by Part II (sections 3–7) of the Trustee Act 2000. The Act gives trustees and personal representatives (who will for the purpose of conciseness both be referred to in this section as 'the trustee') the same powers to invest money as they would have if they owned the monies themselves, but also provides that:

◆ any restrictions or other provisions contained in the will or other document creating the trust, if dated after 3 August 1961, must be complied with;

◆ the trustee has a duty to use such skill and care in the choice of investments and advisers as is reasonable, bearing in mind any special knowledge, experience and professional skill of the trustee and the nature and purpose of the trust;

◆ in the choice of investments a trustee must bear in mind the need for diversification, i.e. he must not put all the eggs in one basket;

◆ the investments should be kept under review with a view to deciding whether or not they should be varied; and

◆ unless it is not appropriate that they should do so or unnecessary, trustees should obtain and consider proper advice as to how the power of investment should be exercised and the suitability of the investments to the trust. It might not be appropriate to take advice if, for example, the trustee himself has the necessary investment skills and knowledge, or if the cost of the advice would be out of proportion to the value of the investments.

Persons of unsound mind

Similarly, if a bequest has been made to a person who is not believed to be of sound mind, the bequest should not be paid to that person personally but to his receiver or to his attorney appointed under lasting power of attorney executed before the beneficiary lost his sanity.

Bankrupts

Payment should not be made to a beneficiary who is bankrupt, and the same points as are noted above on p. 105 in relation to payment of debts to bankrupts apply to payments of entitlements to bankrupt beneficiaries. Before distributing assets check that creditors and beneficiaries are not bankrupt by making a search against their names at the Land Charges Registry on Land Registry form K16 at a current fee of £1.00 for each name searched.

Beneficiaries who cannot *easily* be found

If executors do not personally know a beneficiary's current address, enquiry through persons mentioned in the deceased's address book will sometimes provide the required information. If it does not, then try publishing the statutory advertisement for claimants and creditors referred to on page 92. The addresses of local newspapers can be found by consulting Willing's Press Guide in the reference department of a library or the websites www.wrx.zen.co.uk/norpress.htm and www.wrx.zen.co.uk/soupress.htm.

If the general area in which the missing beneficiary lives is known, a search for the name in the telephone directory or electoral register might find the beneficiary or a member of the family, who will enable contact to be made. Remember to search for married female beneficiaries in both their maiden and married names. A copy of a married woman's marriage certificate, obtainable from the General Registry Office and viewable on the Family Records Centre, will give her maiden name and a lead to the maternal side of the missing beneficiary's family. However, it is possible for a telephone subscriber to elect to be ex-directory and for a registering elector to opt for non-disclosure of the entry contained in the electoral register. If the beneficiary is on the electoral register but has elected for non-disclosure there is the possibility that the local authority will forward a prepaid letter to the relevant address. If the telephone subscribers are not ex-directory their numbers can be searched for on line at www2.bt.com/edq_resname-search.

The Traceline team at The Office for National Statistics (telephone 01514 714811, website www.gro.gov.uk/gro/content) will also trace and forward a letter to anyone who is registered with a National Health Service General Practitioner in England or Wales if the executor can supply the person's name and date of birth. A fee is payable and Traceline can also inform the executor if the beneficiary has died.

Indices of births, adoptions, deaths and marriages from 1837 which may be required can be seen at the Family Records Centre (www.familyrecords.gov.uk/frc) and copy certificates obtained from the General Registry Office (www.gro.gov.uk). Copy probates, Letters of Administration and wills can also provide much useful information. They can be obtained for a modest fee from the Principal Probate Registry.

Professional genealogists and tracing agencies may be employed if the sum involved is large enough to justify the cost, and if all fails the deceased's will should be checked to see if it contains directions as to whether the contingency is provided for. If it does not a solicitor should be instructed to pay the bequest into court or to make an application to a court for directions as to what further should be done.

THE TRANSFER OF CHATTELS

Unless the will provides to the contrary, the cost and risks of delivering a chattel, i.e. a moveable object, to a beneficiary to whom it has been bequeathed, for example the cost of insurance, packing, and transportation, must be borne by the legatee and not by those entitled to the residue of the estate.

If a chattel which has been bequeathed to a specific legatee is not required for the payment of debts or expenses to be incurred in the administration of the estate, the personal representative is under no duty to take other than routine steps to recover it. Thus in the case of Re Clough-Tayor deceased, Coutts & Co. V. Banks and Others, the court decided that executors were under no duty to litigate to recover a chattel that had been taken by a third party following the death of the testatrix and which was not needed for payment of debts or expenses to be incurred in the administration of the estate. The court decided that the executors need do no more than transfer the right to the chattel to the beneficiary in writing.

TRANSFERRING BUILDINGS OR LAND

Leasehold property is special in that the lease under which the property is held sometimes contains provisions requiring the death certificate, probate or letters of administration and a copy of any transfer of the lease to a beneficiary, to be registered with (i.e. produced to), the landlord within specified time limits so that the landlord is kept aware of the identity of his tenant and a fee to be paid to the landlord for the landlord's trouble. In theory failure to register the document with the landlord could result in loss of the lease so the matter should not be overlooked.

When transferring leasehold property care must also be taken to check whether or not there are any outstanding liabilities such as arrears of ground rent or dilapidations under the lease, and reference should be made to the will to decide who should bear them. A personal representative transferring leasehold property to a beneficiary should ensure that the transfer deed contains a provision by the beneficiary to indemnify the personal representative against existing and future dilapidations in respect of the property and to observe and perform the terms of the lease in the future.

Properties have either a registered title or an unregistered title and if the title is not already registered it is necessary to register it whenever a change of ownership takes place, unless the property is leasehold and there is less than seven years before the lease expires.

A registered one is one which has been investigated by The Land Registry and in respect of which The Land Registry has issued one of the following title documents: a Title Information Document, a Land Certificate, or a Charge Certificate. Such documents certify and guarantee the quality and details of the title as at the time they were issued.

If there is no such document with the title documents, it is virtually certain that the title is an unregistered one, but the position must be checked by submitting a search of the Index Map to the relevant District Land Registry. Such a search is free unless more than ten titles are involved, in which case the current fee is £4 for each additional title. In the case of an exceptionally large area of land the Registry can charge an additional fee to reflect the amount of work involved.

The search can be done by post on Land Registry Form number SIM.

Land Registry forms and a note of relevant Land Registry fees can be obtained from The District Land Registry, from a Law Stationer, or downloaded for private use from the Land Registry's website www.landregistry.gov.uk.

The name and address of the relevant District Land Registry appears in the Land Registry document evidencing title and can also be obtained from The Land Registry website.

If the title is not a registered one and the property is to be transferred to a beneficiary or sold, it is necessary to ask The Land Registry to register it, unless the property is leasehold and there is less than seven years before the lease expires.

Preparation of an application to register a title can only be safely done by someone with a considerable knowledge of property law and is best done by a solicitor.

If the title has previously been registered in joint names, on the death of one of the registered owners it is necessary to send a registrar's copy of the death certificate, or official copy of the grant of representation to the estate to the District Land Registry, where the title is registered and quote the title number so that the death can be noted on the registers of the title. No fee is payable.

In any other case, unless the Personal Representatives sell the property and transfer it directly to the purchaser, giving the proceeds to the beneficiary entitled to inherit it (which is the cheaper and quicker course) it will be necessary to prepare a transfer of the property to the beneficiary entitled on the death (or to the trustees of the trust, if a trust comes into existence as a result of the death). The transfer must be registered with The Land Registry and the Land Registry's transfer fee which is based upon the value of the property must be paid.

If the property was owned by one person before his death and does not have a registered title it is better to ask a solicitor to transfer the property and register the transfer and title at the Land Registry at the same time. If the property already has a registered title and is to be transferred to a beneficiary after the death, it is a simple matter to effect the transfer which is done on a Land Registry form number AS1 or AS3. Form AS1 is used if the entirety of the property is to be transferred and form AS3 if only part of the property is to be transferred. The forms should be sent to the relevant District Land Registry with an official copy of the grant of representation, a completed Land Registry Form AP1, and the appropriate Land Registry fee payable by cheque or postal order to 'Land Registry'. If the applicant is aware that the property is occupied by someone other than the beneficiary to whom the property is being transferred, or that there has been any transaction after the date stated on the Land Registry title document, or which is not referred to on the reply to the Search of the Index Map (which transaction affected the property), the applicant cannot safely complete the first box in section 10 of form AP1 and should seek assistance from a solicitor or licensed conveyancer. If the applicant is not aware of any such matters he can tick the first box in section 10 and ignore the second box.

The amount of the relevant fees payable to the Land Registry and the Land Registry forms can be obtained from the Registry or downloaded for private use from the Land Registry website.

If registered land is mortgaged, when the mortgage is paid off, the lender will either notify the Land Registry electronically that the mortgage has been paid off, or supply the person to whom it sends the deeds with an acknowledgement that the mortgage has been paid off in the form of a completed Land Registry Form DS1. To remove the reference to the mortgage from the property title the form of application which is on the back of Form DS1 should be completed and sent to the relevant District Land Registry with a completed Form AP1 or DS2 and the original Grant of Representation to the estate. No fee is payable.

The Land Registry website includes an online enquiry form and a section of frequently asked questions and answers.

TRANSFERRING SHARES OR STOCK
The steps to be taken are described on page 102.

CAPITAL GAINS TAX AND INCOME TAX EARNED DURING THE ADMINISTRATION PERIOD
If the estate assets rise in value between the date of death and the date they are transferred to beneficiaries or the date they

are cashed or, if they produce income, the personal representatives and the estate must account to the Revenue for any chargeable Income and Capital Gains Tax.

Capital Gains Tax

Personal representatives are entitled to the deceased's personal Capital Gains Tax exemption limit in the tax year in which death takes place and in the two tax years which follow death. Assets which have a large capital gain should therefore usually be dealt with by transfer to beneficiaries or sale within three years of death, if possible, although careful consideration of the amount of the gain with which each asset is pregnant, the taper relief applicable to it and spacing of sales over the three tax years can prove advantageous. When deciding whether to sell assets or transfer them to the beneficiaries and let the beneficiary sell them, the personal representative should take into account the beneficiary's views and Capital Gains Tax position and the current Capital Gains Tax rates for individuals and for personal representatives, with a view to acting in the way which will prove to be the more favourable. The personal representative's Capital Gains Tax exemption and that of the beneficiary are independent of each other; careful use of both of them can achieve considerable tax savings if the gains since death are large.

Losses which occur in the year of death can be carried back for Capital Gains Tax purposes and used to reduce gains which occurred in the three years which preceded death.

When Personal Representatives or beneficiaries sell or dispose of assets inherited from an estate then for Capital Gains Tax purposes when calculating the gain, they are allowed to add to the base cost (i.e. the cost at which they are deemed to have acquired the relevant asset), a proportion of the legal and other expenses involved in preparing the Inland Revenue account and obtaining the grant of probate.

Because it is difficult to ascertain exactly how much of the total expense relates to any particular asset a scale (known as 'The Richards Scale') is usually accepted. The scale used for deaths which take place after 5 April 1993 is:

Gross value of the estate for IHT purposes	Sum allowed
(a) Up to £40,000	1.75 per cent of the probate value of the asset.
(b) £40,001–£70,000	£700 divided proportionately between the estate assets according to their probate values.
(c) £70,001–£300,000	1 per cent of the probate value of the asset.
(d) £300,001–£400,000	£3,000 divided proportionately between the estate assets according to their probate values.
(e) £400,001–£750,000	0.75 per cent of the probate value of the asset.

Also bear in mind that if assets are re-valued for Inheritance Tax purposes to reflect a fall in value between the date of death and the date they are transferred to the beneficiary or sold, then for Capital Gains Tax purposes the reduced value becomes the base cost value (i.e. the value at which the asset is deemed to have been acquired by the beneficiary) and before deciding to elect for an Inheritance Tax revaluation, check whether Inheritance Tax and Capital Gains Tax are at the same rates at the relevant time.

When passing a bequest to a beneficiary a Personal Representative should retain a sufficient sum from the bequest to meet any potential Capital Gains Tax liability if the Capital Gains Tax position has not been finally agreed with the Revenue.

Income tax

Income is taxed in the hands of the personal representatives on the basis of the tax year in which it is due and not the tax year in which it is actually received; it is not apportioned over the period before and the period after death. The personal representatives are entitled to set against the gross income they receive from the administration of the estate during a tax year any interest they pay during that tax year on loans they have taken out to finance the payment of inheritance tax.

Some of the income earned by assets of the estate between death and distribution of the estate may have been taxed at source (i.e. before it was paid to the estate), but other income such as rent and interest on a company debenture is paid to the personal representatives without any deduction of tax. This is taxable at the standard rate in the hands of the personal representatives to whom no personal allowances are available.

Each beneficiary must include his share of the income of the estate earned between death and distribution of the estate in his tax return, but he is entitled to credit for tax paid by the personal representatives on the share. Beneficiaries who are not liable for income tax can reclaim tax which has been deducted at source or which has been paid by the personal representatives in respect of the beneficiary's share of income. Higher rate tax-payers are liable for the difference between the standard and higher rates of tax.

To enable the beneficiaries to deal with the tax and income, the personal representatives must complete for each beneficiary affected a short form (number R185E, obtainable from the local Income Tax Office) which will show the beneficiary's share of the tax and the income.

FINAL ACCOUNTS

Finally, before distributing the estate to the beneficiaries, the personal representative would be well advised to get accounts approved by the residuary beneficiaries and to get a form of receipt and discharge from all the beneficiaries. If the beneficiaries will not sign the form of discharge the personal representatives can make an application for a formal discharge to a court.

It should be noted here that an executor is not entitled to charge for the work he has done or the time he has expended in connection with the estate unless the will provides to the contrary, but he is entitled to be reimbursed for out-of-pocket expenses he has incurred.

A suitable form of account and receipt for the estate outlined on pages 70 and 71 might be as follows:

ESTATE ACCOUNTS RELATING TO THE ESTATE OF THE LATE A.A.B.

A.A.B. died on 30 January 2006 having appointed his sons A.B. and C.B. to be the executors of his last will dated 22 June 2002. By the will A.A.B. devised his house 23 Church Street Hove Sussex to his son A.B. and after leaving legacies of £10,000.00 to each of his friends E.F. and I.J., A.A.B. gave the remainder of his estate to his son C.B. and his daughter K.L. in equal shares. I.J. predeceased the testator on 2 November 2002. The executors proved the will in the Brighton District Probate Registry on 22 March 2006.

CASH ACCOUNT

	£
23 Church Street Hove Sussex transferred to A.B.	180,000.00
Furniture and effects	15,000.00
Of Big Insurance Co. – proceeds of life policy	10,000.00
Of Barclays Bank Plc. – balance on current account	300.00
Of Nationwide Building Society – balance on account	1290.10
Of Yorkshire Building Society – balance on account	6709.90
Of Nationwide Building Society – balance on ISA account	12,000.00
By encashment of Premium Savings Bonds	700.00
By encashment of Pensioners Bonds	2,000.00
Cash in house	100.00
Shares in Tesco Plc	1,020.50
Shares in Northern Rock Plc	2,205.00
Shares in Severn Trent Water	1,005.50
Shares in British Energy Plc	1,669.00
Interest between death and closure on building society accounts	60.50
Interest between death and closure on Pensioners Bonds	20.00
Dividend received since death	15.50
Gain on shares sold during the administration of the estate	80.20
Total	234,176.20

Deduct	£
Income tax	4.00
Funeral account and post-funeral meal	1,400.00

Probate fees	400.00	
Cost of statutory advertisement for creditors	117.50	
HM Land Registry fee on transfer of house	50.00	
Executor's expenses and cost of death certificates	76.00	2,047.50
Balance carried to Distribution Account		232,128.70

DISTRIBUTION ACCOUNT

	£	£
Balance from Cash Account		232,128.70
Less:		
To A.B. bequest of 23 Church Street Hove	180,000.00	
To E.F. legacy	10,000.00	
To C.B. ½ share of residue	21,064.35	
To K.L. ½ share of residue	21,064.35	232,128.70

We A.B., E.F., C.B. and K.L. approve and agree the above accounts and acknowledge that we have received from A.B. and C.B., the executors of the estate, the above bequests in full satisfaction of all claims by us against the estate and the executors of the will.

Signed by A.B. this   day of   2006

_____

Signed by E.F. this   day of   2006

_____

Signed by C.B. this   day of   2006

_____

Signed by K.L. this   day of   2006

_____

Before submitting the accounts for the approval of the beneficiaries, care should be taken to reconcile the accounts with the bank statements by ensuring that the balance of the Cash Account, after making allowances for anything transferred to beneficiaries without being turned into cash, agrees with the final sum withdrawn from the bank account. If it does not there must be an error in the bank statement or, more likely, an omission from or other error in the estate accounts.

Appendix 1

Specimen Forms and Letters

SPECIMEN FORM OF LIVING WILL

1. I (*insert your full names, address and occupation, if any*), on the (*insert the date*) make this Living Will and set down as guidance to my family and my medical practitioners these advance directions as to the types of medical treatment I wish and do not wish to undergo even if my life is at risk and bearing in mind that in the future I might be unable to express my wishes.

2. IN giving these directions I consider that:

   ◆ I am in good physical health

   ◆ I am mentally competent

   ◆ I have considered the matter thoroughly

   ◆ I believe myself to be fully informed and

   ◆ I do so voluntarily and free from influence by others.

3. IF any of the conditions specified in the First Schedule below apply to me and in the opinion of (*insert number*) ▶

medical practitioners I am unlikely to recover a good quality of life THEN I would not wish to undergo any of the treatments specified in the Second Schedule below, but would wish attempts to be made to prolong my life by the treatments specified in the Third Schedule below if they are appropriate.

The First Schedule referred to above – the conditions

- I am brain dead.

- I show no signs of cerebral activity.

- I am suffering from permanent mental impairment.

- I have been in a continuous coma for (*insert the number*) of months.

- By reason of mental illness I have been unable to recognise and respond to my family or friends and I have not been aware of my surroundings or able to differentiate between night and day for (*insert the number*) of months.

- I am suffering from any degenerative and incurable illness.

- I am so disabled that I am completely dependent upon others and my condition is unlikely to improve.

- I have suffered (*insert the number*) cardiac arrests.

- I am totally paralysed.

- I am blind, dumb and deaf.

- I am in a persistent vegetative state.

The Second Schedule referred to above – treatment I do not wish to have

- Attempted resuscitation.

- Artificial feeding or hydration.

- Drug therapy.

- Blood transfusions.

- Artificial ventilation.

- Treatment in connection with which the risks are high compared with the likely benefits.

The Third Schedule referred to above – treatment I wish to have if appropriate

- Artificial feeding or hydration.

- Attempted resuscitation.

- Drug therapy.

- Blood transfusions.

- Artificial ventilation.

- Treatment to alleviate pain notwithstanding that it might shorten my life.

▶

SIGNED by me (*insert your full names*)
(*Sign your name here*)

In the presence of (*insert full names of the witness*)
(*Witness to sign and print full names and address here*)

Note. The conditions and treatments set out in the schedules are specimens only and may be added to, omitted or varied, but any attempt to prevent basic care such as feeding by mouth or washing will be ineffective.

WORKSHEET

Personal Details

Full name of deceased

Usual address at death

Address in will

Occupation

Marital status

Date of birth

Date of death

Surviving relatives – husband/wife – brother(s)/
sister(s) – parents – children
Name
Number of:
  – children
  – grandchildren

National Insurance number

Income tax district and reference

Date of will

Domicile

Full names and addresses and occupations of executors

Substantial gifts made in the last seven years?

Progress schedule

Date of grant of probate

Date of publication of advertisement for claimants

Expiry date for claims

Date inheritance tax clearance application dispatched

Date inheritance tax clearance received

Employees?

Household insurance policies

Date notified   Effected   Cancelled

Items to be returned to owners, date returned

Interest in trusts?

Estate assets

Asset	Date death notified	Date grant registered	Date asset realised	Sum received

Estate Liabilities

Creditor	Date death notified	Date debt paid

Legacies

Legatee's name	Current address	Amount or asset	Date paid or transferred

Estate accounts

Residuary beneficiary's name	Date submitted for approval	Date approved	Date distribution made

ADVERTISEMENT FOR CREDITORS AND CLAIMANTS WHERE THERE IS A WILL – LOCAL NEWSPAPER

Advertisement pursuant to Section 27 of The Trustee Act 1925 – (*insert name*) Deceased.

NOTICE IS HEREBY GIVEN pursuant to Section 27 of The Trustee Act 1925 that any person having a claim against or interest in the estate of (*insert full names*) who died on the (*insert date*) and whose will appointed (*insert executors' names and addresses*) to be the executors thereof are required to send particulars in writing of their claim to the executors by the (*insert date to be at least two months after the date of the publication of the notice*) after which date the executors will distribute the estate among the persons entitled thereto having regard only to the claims and interests of which they have then had notice.

DATED this   day of   2006

Signed   and

Executors

ADVERTISEMENT FOR CREDITORS AND CLAIMANTS WHERE THERE IS NO WILL – LOCAL NEWSPAPER

Advertisement pursuant to Section 27 of The Trustee Act 1925 – (*insert name*) Deceased.

NOTICE IS HEREBY GIVEN pursuant to Section 27 of The Trustee Act 1925 that any person having a claim against or interest in the estate of (*insert full names*) who died on the (*insert date*) are required to send particulars in writing of their claim to (*insert names and addresses of the proposed personal representatives*) the proposed administrators of the estate by the (*insert date to be at least two months after the date of the publication of the notice*) after which date the administrators will distribute the estate among the persons entitled thereto having regard only to the claims and interests of which they have then had notice.

DATED this   day of   2006

Signed   and

Proposed Administrators of the Estate.

LETTER TO ACCOMPANY ADVERTISEMENT FOR CREDITORS AND CLAIMANTS – LOCAL NEWSPAPER

To (*insert name and address of newspaper*)

Dear Sirs

(*insert name of deceased*) Deceased
I enclose advertisement pursuant to section 27 of The Trustee Act 1925 and I shall be obliged if you will arrange for its publication, once only please, in the first possible issue of (*insert name of newspaper*).
Please let me have a voucher copy of the publication and your account in due course.

Yours faithfully

TO *THE LONDON GAZETTE* REQUESTING FORM FOR ADVERTISEMENT FOR CLAIMANTS AND CREDITORS

To the Manager
The London Gazette
PO Box 7923
London SE1 5ZH

Dear Sir,

I shall be obliged if you will let me have a form for completion to enable me to have an advertisement published in *The Gazette* pursuant to section 27 of The Trustee Act 1925 and a note of the fee payable.

Yours faithfully

TO *THE LONDON GAZETTE* ENCLOSING FORM FOR ADVERTISEMENT FOR CLAIMANTS AND CREDITORS

To the Manager
The London Gazette
PO Box 7923
London SE1 5ZH

Dear Sir

Advertisement pursuant to section 27 of
The Trustee Act 1925
(*insert name of the deceased*)

Please find enclosed

1. Advertisement for claimants and creditors.

2. Office copy grant of representation for inspection and return.

3. Cheque in the sum of (*insert amount*) which I understand to be the correct fee.

Please publish the advertisement in the first possible issue of the *Gazette* and let me have a voucher copy of the advertisement for my records when it has been published.

Yours faithfully

PRE-GRANT OF REPRESENTATION LETTERS

To banks and building societies

The Manager
(*insert name of Society or Bank*)
(*insert address*)

Dear Sir

I am the executor of the will of your customer (*insert name of the deceased*) of (*insert address*) who died on (*insert date of death*) and I enclose a registrar's death certificate and a copy of the will for noting in your records and return.

Please let me have details of all accounts which the deceased has with your organisation, and particulars of any assets or securities held for the estate.

In respect of each account please state:

1. the balance of the account as at the date of death including accrued interest

2. the interest accrued to the account between the end of the last financial year and the date of death

3. whether the interest is gross or net and if net the amount of tax deducted and

4. whether there are any direct debits or standing orders in respect of the account and if so kindly supply me with full particulars.

I shall be obliged if you will also let me know your requirements to close the accounts and let me have any necessary forms for signature.

▶

For reasons of security I have destroyed the deceased's (*insert bank or building society as appropriate*) card(s) number(s) (*insert numbers*).

Please cancel any standing orders in respect of the accounts and do not meet any more direct debits.

All future communications should be sent to me at my above address.

Yours faithfully

Note. If a passbook is available, insert the following additional paragraph after the first paragraph. 'The passbook for account number (*insert number*) is enclosed to be made up to date and returned to me please.'

To Pep or Isa Manager

To The Manager

(*insert name and address of the management Company*)

Dear Sirs,

(*Insert name of the deceased, client or customer number or reference and name of the trust, if known*)

I regret to inform you that the above unit holder died on (*insert date of death*).

I am the executor of the deceased's will and enclose a Registrar's copy of his death certificate and a copy of his will, both for your inspection and return.

To enable me to complete the papers to obtain a grant of representation to the estate, please confirm the holding and let me know its value for inheritance tax purposes as at the date of death.

If you are aware of any other holdings of the deceased under your management please let me have details of them.

To enable me to complete the tax return to the date of death, kindly let me have details of any distributions made in respect of the holdings in the current tax year.

Please let me know your requirements to enable the holding to be realised in due course and send me any necessary forms for completion.

All future correspondence should be sent to me at the above address.

Yours faithfully,

To Benefits Agency

The Benefits Agency
(*insert address*)

Dear Sirs

(*insert name*) deceased
National Insurance number (*insert number*)

I am the executor of the will of (*insert name of the above named deceased*) of (*insert address*) who died on (*insert date of death*) and I enclose a registrar's death certificate and a copy of the will for noting in your records and return.

Please also find enclosed the deceased's pension (*insert book or card as appropriate*).

Kindly let me know the amount of any benefit which the agency claims has been overpaid so that repayment can be made when the estate is in funds or the amount of any outstanding benefit due to the estate. Please also let me know your requirements to enable payment of any outstanding benefit to be made.

All future communications should be sent to me at my above address.

Yours faithfully

To company registrars in respect of shares and/or stock

The Registrar
(*insert company name and address of the registrar*)

Dear Sir

The late (*insert name*)
(*insert company name and share account number,
if known*)

I am the personal representative of (*insert deceased's name*) and I enclose a death certificate for registration in your books and return.

Please let me have (*insert number of transfer deeds required*) transfer deeds for completion to enable me to transfer the holding to the beneficiaries when the grant of representation, which will be registered with you, is to hand.

Yours faithfully

To creditors

To (*insert name and address of creditor*)

Dear Sir

Account Number (*insert number*)

I am the executor of the will of (*insert name of the deceased*) of (*insert address*) who died on (*insert date of death*) and I enclose a registrar's death certificate for noting in your records and return.

Please let me have a final statement detailing the amount claimed and in view of the death, see that no enforcement action is taken until the estate is in funds.

All future correspondence should be sent to me at the above address.

Yours faithfully

Note. If the creditor is a credit or debit card company add, 'I am destroying the card number (*insert number*) to avoid it being misused'.

To employer

To (*insert name and address of employer*)

For the attention of the Salaries Department

Dear Sirs

(*insert name*) deceased, employee number
(*insert number*)

I am the executor of the will of (*insert name of the deceased*) of (*insert address*) who died on (*insert date of death*) and was employed by the company as a (*insert job title*) in the (*insert name of department*) department. A registrar's death certificate and a copy of the will are enclosed for noting in your records and return.

Please let me know:

1. Whether there are any arrears of salary or other payments due to the estate (and if so the amounts involved) and your requirements to enable them to be claimed.

2. The gross amount of salary payable in the current tax year and the deductible amount of income tax.

3. Whether to your knowledge, your late employee was a member of any pension fund and if so the name and address of the fund and the membership number.

Yours faithfully

To household insurance companies

To the Manager
(*insert name and address of company*)

Dear Sir

Policy number (*insert number*)

I am the executor of the will of (*insert name of the deceased*) of (*insert address*) who was the holder of the above policy and who died on (*insert date of death*). A registrar's death certificate is enclosed for noting in your records and return.

The property is currently furnished but unoccupied and as executor I wish to keep the insurance in force pending clearance of the effects and disposal of the property which will take place following the issue of a formal grant of representation to the estate. Please let me know your requirements to enable this to be done.

All future communications should be sent to me at my above address.

Yours faithfully

To Inland Revenue concerning income and capital gains tax

To HM Inspector of Taxes
(*insert name and address of inspector*)

Tax reference (*insert if known*)

Dear Sir

I am the executor of the will of (*insert name of the deceased*) of (*insert address*) who died on (*insert date of death*) and I enclose a registrar's death certificate and a copy of the will for noting in your records and return.

Please supply me with a copy of the deceased's last tax return and the appropriate forms to enable me to make a return to the date of death and in due course a personal representative's return for the period to the finalisation of the estate.

Please also let me have details of any tax now outstanding or any repayment due to the estate and the Revenue's requirements to enable these matters to be dealt with.

All future communications should be sent to me at my above address.

Yours faithfully

To life assurance company

To (*insert name and address of company*)

Dear Sirs

Policy number (*insert policy number*)

I am the executor of the will of your customer (*insert name of the deceased*) of (*insert address*) who died on (*insert date of death*) and I enclose a registrar's death certificate and a copy of the will for noting in your records and return. The original policy and premium book are also enclosed.

Please let me know:

1. your requirements to enable the policy monies to be paid;

2. whether you know of any other policies on the deceased's life with your company; and

3. the sum(s) payable in respect of each policy specifying interest payable separately.

Yours faithfully

To mortgage company

To the Manager
(*insert name and address of company*)

Dear Sir,

> (*insert mortgage account reference number and address of the property mortgaged*)
> (*insert name of the deceased*)

I am the executor of the will of your above named customer late of (*insert address*) who died on (*insert date of death*) and I enclose a registrar's death certificate and a copy of the will for noting in your records and return.

Please note the death in your records and let me know the amount of the capital outstanding in respect of the mortgage as at the date of the death and the date the mortgage was effected.

Kindly also let me know the amount of interest outstanding at the date of death.

If the mortgage was supported by a life or endowment policy, please let me have details of the policy including the name and current address of the company concerned and the policy number.

The grant of representation will be registered with you when it is to hand and at that date I shall let you know whether it is desired to pay off the mortgage or whether a request will be made to continue it in the beneficiary's name. Until that date please see that no enforcement action is taken.

Yours faithfully

To National Savings Bank

To the Director of Savings
National Savings Bank
Glasgow
G58 1SB

Dear Sir

I am the executor of the will of (*insert name of the deceased*) of (*insert address*) who was the holder of account number (*insert account number*) and who died on (*insert date of death*). The passbook is enclosed together with a registrar's death certificate and copy of the will all for noting in your records and return.

Please make the book up to date and let me know the amount of interest accrued in the current tax year to the date of death.

When replying, kindly let me have the appropriate form to close the account.

All future communications should be sent to me at my above address.

Yours faithfully

To National Savings Certificates

The Director of Savings
Savings Certificates Division
Durham
DH99 1NS

Dear Sir

I am the executor of the will of (*insert name of the deceased*) of (*insert address*) who was the holder of the certificates described below and who died on (*insert date of death*). The holder's number is (*insert the number*). A registrar's death certificate and copy of the will are enclosed for noting in your records and return.

Please let me have a note of the value of the certificates as at the date of death and the appropriate form for me to (*insert transfer or cash as is required*) the certificates when the grant of representation is to hand.

All future communications should be sent to me at my above address.

Yours faithfully

Certificate number (*insert numbers*) dated (*insert dates*) for (*insert number of units in the particular certificate*).

Paragraph to be inserted in pre-grant letters to organisations from which money is due if the gross value of the estate is under £5,000:

> In view of the fact that it is not anticipated that the gross value of the estate will exceed £5,000 and in order to keep expenses in proportion, it is not proposed to extract a grant of representation to the estate unless you insist.

To pension fund when pension is already being paid

The Secretary
(*insert pension fund name and address*)

Dear Sirs

(*insert name*) deceased Pension number (*insert number*)

I am the executor of the will of your pensioner (*insert name of the deceased*) of (*insert address*) who died on (*insert date of death*) and I enclose a registrar's death certificate and a copy of the will for noting in your records and return.

Please let me know:

1. whether there are any arrears of pension due to the estate to the date of death or any overpaid pension due to be refunded to the pension fund;

2. your requirements to enable you to pay any arrears;

3. the gross amount of pension payable in the current tax year, including sums due to the date of death but not yet paid;

4. the amount of tax deducted or which will be deducted from the current tax year's pension; and

5. the address and reference number for the relevant tax district.

All future communications should be sent to me at my above address.

Yours faithfully

To pension fund when pension is not yet being paid

The Secretary
(*insert pension fund name and address*)

Dear Sirs

> (*insert name*) deceased Pension number (*insert number if known*)

I am the executor of the will of (*insert name of the deceased*) of *(insert address)* who died on (*insert date of death*).

I understand that the deceased, who was employed by (*insert employer's name*) at (*insert address at which employed*), was a member of your scheme.

A registrar's death certificate and a copy of the will are enclosed for noting in your records and return, and I shall be obliged if you will let me know what benefits are due to the deceased's estate and dependants and whether the benefits are subject to inheritance tax.

Yours faithfully

To supply companies

To the Accounts Manager
(*insert name and address of company*)

Dear Sir

Account number (*insert number*)

I am the executor of the will of your customer (*insert name of the deceased*) of (*insert address*) who died on (*insert date of death*) and I enclose a registrar's death certificate for noting in your records and return.

Please confirm the sum claimed to the date of death and in view of the death see that no enforcement action is taken until the estate is in funds and payment can be made.

I wish to continue the supply until further notice and shall be obliged if you will let me know your requirements to enable this to be done.

All future correspondence should be sent to me at the above address.

Yours faithfully

To trustees of a trust of which the deceased was a life tenant or annuitant

---

(insert name and address of the trustees)

Dear Sir

(insert the name of the trust)

I am the executor of the will of *(insert name of the deceased)* of *(insert address)* who died on *(insert date of death)* and I enclose a registrar's death certificate and a copy of the will for noting in your records and return.

My information is that the deceased was a beneficiary of the trust and I shall be obliged if you will let me have a copy of the trust instrument and particulars of the trust fund for my information.

Please let me know the gross and net income due to the estate to the date of death.

Yours faithfully

POST-GRANT OF REPRESENTATION

To registrars in respect of shares and/or stock

The Registrar
(*insert company name and address*)

Dear Sir

The late (*insert name and account number of holding if known*)

I am the personal representative of (*insert deceased's name*) and I enclose an office copy of the grant of representation for registration and return, and the relevant certificates together with the uncashed (*insert dividend or interest as appropriate*) warrant(s) in respect of the holdings set out below.

Please amend or reissue the warrants in my name so that they can be paid into the estate's bank account (*insert 'and let me have new certificates in accordance with the enclosed transfer deeds' or insert 'and endorse the certificates so that I can arrange to sell the holdings' as required*).

Yours faithfully

Enclosures:

Office copy grant of representation.

(*insert company name*) certificate number (*insert number*) in respect of (*insert number in the case of shares or amount of stock in the case of loan or debenture stock*) of (*insert description of security, e.g. 25p ordinary shares or 1st Debenture stock*).

▶

(*Insert company name*) (*insert dividend or interest as appropriate*) warrant dated (*insert date*) for (*insert amount*).

(If the security is to be transferred add '(*insert company name*) transfer deed in respect of (*insert holding to be transferred*) in favour of (*insert name of new holder*)'.

To stock brokers in respect of shares and/or stock held in broker's nominee account

To

(*insert broker's name and address*)

Dear Sirs,

The late (*insert name and account number of holding if known*)

I am the personal representative of (*insert deceased's name*) and I enclose an office copy of the grant of representation for registration and return in respect of the deceased's holding in (*insert the name of the relevant company*).

Please *transfer/sell* the holdings as follows (*set out the details of the required transfers or sales for each company stating the relevant number of shares or amount of stock, and name and address of each transferee if transfers are required*).

Yours faithfully

Enclosures:

Office copy grant of representation.

To creditor paying account

> To (*insert name and address of company*)
>
> Dear Sirs
>
>   The estate of the late (*insert name of the deceased*)
>
> I send herewith a cheque in the sum of £(*insert amount*) in settlement of your enclosed account. Please return it to me marked as paid at your early convenience.
>
> Yours faithfully

To Inspector of Taxes notifying end of administration period and enclosing final tax return

HM Inspector of Taxes
(*insert address of relevant tax office*)

Tax Reference (*insert reference*)

Dear Sir

The estate of the late (*insert name of the deceased*)

No further income is anticipated in respect of the above estate and I enclose the final tax return in respect of the estate, together with the certificates of deduction of tax from the income. Please return the certificates to me when they have served your purposes.

Please also accept this letter as formal notice that the administration period in respect of the above estate ended on (*insert the date when all the assets and liabilities of the estate were known, no further income was anticipated and the liabilities had been paid and discharged*) and let me have a final tax assessment in respect of the estate.

I shall be obliged if you will also let me have (*insert the number required, one for each beneficiary entitled to income from the estate and for each tax year of the administration period*) forms R185E.

Yours faithfully

**To Inland Revenue requesting Inheritance Tax Clearance
certificate**

To Capital Taxes
Farrers House
PO Box 38
Castle Meadow Road
Nottingham
NG2 1BB

Dear Sirs

> Your Reference (*insert Capital Taxes reference*)
> The estate of the late (*insert name of the deceased*)
> Date of death (*insert date*)

I shall be obliged if you will let me have a formal
Inheritance Tax Clearance certificate at your early
convenience.

Yours faithfully

To residuary beneficiaries enclosing accounts for approval

To (*insert name and address of beneficiary*)

Dear

    The estate of the late (*insert name of the deceased*)

I believe that I have now completed the administration of the estate and I enclose copies of the accounts in duplicate for your approval and I have similarly sent copies of the accounts to the other parties involved for their approval.

If you approve the accounts, please sign and date the form of discharge at the bottom of one copy of the accounts and return that copy to me.

When all parties have returned the accounts to me approved I shall be in a position to let you have a remittance for the sum shown as due to you by the accounts.

If you have any queries on the accounts I shall be pleased to deal with them upon hearing from you.

Yours faithfully

Form of receipt for legacy

> The estate of the late (*insert deceased's name*)
>
> I, (*insert name of beneficiary*) of (*insert address and if different from that stated in the will add 'formerly of' and the address stated in the will*) acknowledge that I have received from (*insert your name*) the personal representative of the late (*insert the deceased's name*) (*insert description of the bequest following the description given in the will as far as possible*) in full satisfaction of my entitlement from the estate.
>
> Dated
>
> Signed

Appendix 2

Useful addresses

Association of British Insurers, 51 Gresham Street, London EC2V 7HQ. Tel: 020 7600 3333. www.abi.org.uk

British Bankers Association, Pinners Hall, 105 –108 Old Broad Street, London EC2A 1EX. Tel: 020 7216 8800. www.bba.org.uk

British Humanist Association, 1 Gower Street, London, WC1E 6HD. Tel: 020 7079 3580.

Building Society's Association, 3 Savile Row, London W1S 3PB. Tel: 020 7437 0655. Fax: 020 7734 6416. www.bsa.org.uk

Capital Taxes Office, Farrers House, PO Box 38, Castle Meadow Road, Nottingham NG2 1BB. Tel: 0845 3020900. www.hmrc.gov.uk/cto

Charity Commission, Harmsworth House, 13–15 Bouverie Street, London EC4Y 8DP. Tel: 45 300 0218. Fax: 020 7674 2300. www.charity-commission.gov.uk

Compakta Limited, Environ, Parkfield, Western Park, Hinkley Road, Leicester LE3 6HX. Tel and fax: 01162 333 566

Computershare Investor Services Plc., P.O. Box 82, The Pavilions, Bridgwater Road, Bristol BS99 7NH. Tel: 087 0702 0002. Fax: 087 0703 6101.

Coroners Section, Home Office, 5th Floor, Allington Towers, 19 Allington Street, London SW1E 5EB. Tel: 020 7340 6659/6660. Fax: 020 7035 5525.

FACTS Health Centre, 23–25 Weston Park, Crouch End, London N8 9SY.

Family Records Centre, 1 Myddleton Street, London EC1R 1UW. Tel: 0845 603 7788. Fax: 01704 550013. www.familyrecords.gov.uk/frc

Financial Services Authority, 25 The North Colonnade, Canary Wharf, London E14 5HS. Tel: 0845 606 1234. www.fsa.gov.uk

Foreign and Commonwealth Office, King Charles Street, London SW1A 2AH. Tel: 020 7008 0186.

FT Information Services, Castle House, 37–45 Paul Street, London EC2A 4LS. Tel: 020 7825 8000. www.ft.com

Funeral Standards Council, 30 North Road, Cardiff, CF1 3DY. Tel: 029 2038 2046.

General Registry Office Certificates Section, The Office for National Statistics, P.O. Box 2, Southport, PR8 2JD. email: certificateservices@ons.qsi.gov.uk. Fax: 01704 550013. Tel: 0845 603 7788. Website: www.gro.gov.uk

General Registry Office Overseas Section, Smedleys Hydro, Trafalgar Road, Birkdale, Southport, PR8 2HH. Tel: 0151 471 4801. Fax: 01633 652988.

H.M. Inspector of Anatomy, Department of Health, Wellington House, 133–155 Waterloo Road, London SE1 8UG. Tel: 020 7972 4342. www.doh.gov.uk/hmia

Inland Revenue Helpline for Probate and Inheritance Tax queries. Tel: 0845 3020900.

Inland Revenue Website www.hmrc.gov.uk

Inquest Charitable Trust, 89–93 Fonthill Road, London N4 3JH. Tel: 020 7263 1111. Fax: 020 7561 0799. email: inquest@inquest.org.uk. Website: www.inquest.org.uk

Land Registry, Lincolns Inn Fields, London, WC2A 3PH. Tel: 020 7917 8888. Fax: 020 7955 0110. www.landregistry.gov.uk

Law stationers – Oyez Straker. see website for local retail shops. Tel: 0870 737 7370. www.oyezformslink.co.uk

Law stationers – Shaw & Sons, Shaway House, 21 Bourne Park Road, Crayford, Kent DA1 4BZ. Tel: 01322 621100. www.shaws.co.uk

Law stationers – Stat Plus, Stat Plus House, Greenlea Park, Prince George's Road, London SW19 2PU. Tel: 020 8646 5500. Fax: 020 8640 2905. www.statplus.co.uk

London Anatomy Office, Imperial College Faculty of Medicine, Charing Cross Hospital, Fulham Palace Road, London W6 8RF. Tel: 020 8846 1216.

London Gazette, PO Box 7923, London SE1 5ZH. Tel: 0870 600 3322. www.gazettes-online.co.uk; email: gazette@tso.co.uk

London Lighthouse Trust, 111–117 Lancaster Road, London W11 1QT. Tel: 020 7792 1200. Fax: 020 7229 1258. email: info@tht.org.uk (now incorporated in The Terrence Higgins Trust).

London Stock Exchange Historic Prices Service, 10 Paternoster Square, London EC4N 7LS. Tel: 0207 797 1206. e-mail: products@londonstockexchange.com. Fax: 0207 797 1952. website: www.londonstockexchange.com/en-gb/products

Mailing Preference Service, D.M.A. House, 70 Margaret Street, London W1W 8SS. Tel: 0845 703 4599. Fax: 020 7323 4226. email: mps@dma.org.uk. Website: www.mpsonline.org.uk

National Asssociation for Widows, 3rd Floor, 48 Queens Road, Coventry. Tel: 0845 838 2261. www.nawidows.org.uk

National Association of Funeral Directors, 618 Warwick Road, Solihull, West Midlands B91 1AA, Tel: 0121 711 1343. www.nafd.org.uk

National Savings and Investments, Tel: 0845 964 5000. Website: www.nasandi.com

National Savings for Fixed Interest Savings, Index Linked Savings Certificates, Cash Mini Isas, Deposit Bonds, Fixed Rate Savings Bonds, S.A.Y.E., Tessa Isas and Yearly Plan. National Savings and Investments, Milburn House, Durham, DH99 1NS. Tel: 0845 964 5000. Website: www.nasandi.com

National Savings for Guaranteed Equity Bonds, Income Bonds, Pensioners Guaranteed Income Bonds and Premium Savings Bonds. National Savings and Investments, Marton Road, Blackpool FY3 9YP Tel: 0845 964 5000. Website: www.nasandi.com

National Savings Tracing, National Savings Tracing Office, Freepost BJ 2092, Blackpool FY3 YP. Tel: 0845 964 5000. www.nsandi.com/help/tracingservice.jsp

Natural Death Centre, 6 Blackstock Mews, Blackstock Road, London N4 2BT. Tel: 0871 288 2098. Fax: 020 7354 3831. www.naturaldeath.org.uk

Pensions Registry Scheme, The Pensions Regulator, Napier House, Trafalgar Place, Brighton BN1 4DW Tel: 01273 627 600. Fax: 01273 627 688. Website: www.thepensionsregulator.gov.uk

Peterborough District Hospital Department of Histology, Peterborough District Hospital, 3 Thorpe Road, Peterborough, PE3 6DA. Tel: 01733 874000. www.tissuebank.co.uk

Probate Department, Principal Registry of The Family Division, 42–49 High Holborn, London WC1V 6NP. Tel: 020 7947 6000 (Record Keeper 020 7947 7000).

The Pensions Tracing Service, Department of Work and Pensions. Tyneview Park, Whitley Road, Newcastle upon Tyne, NE98 1BA. Fax: 0845 3000 169. Website: www.thepensionservice.gov.uk

The Probate and Inheritance Tax Helpline (run by the Capital Taxes Office jointly with The Court Services). Tel: 0845 3020 9000.

The Registry of Shipping and Seamen, Anchor House 12 Cheviot Close, Parc – Ty-Glas, Llanishen, Cardiff CF14 5JA. Tel: 02920 768200.

The Terrence Higgins Trust, 52–54 Grays Inn Road, London WC1X 8JU. Tel: 020 7831 0330 Direct Helpline 0485 1221 200. Fax: 020 7816 4552. Email: info@tht.org.uk. Website: www.tht.org.uk

Traceline, P.O. Box 106, Southport, PR8 2WA. Tel: 0151 4714811. Website: www.gro.gov.uk/gro/content

UK Transplant, Fox Den Road, Stoke Gifford, Bristol, BS34 8RR. Tel: 0117 975 7575. Fax: 0117 975 7577. Website: www.uktransplant.org.uk

The Veterans Agency, Norcross, Blackpool FY5 3WP. Tel: 0800 169 2277.
  www.veteransagency.mod.uk
Vic Fern Company Limited, Crabtree Mill, Hempshill Lane, Bulwell,
  Nottingham, NG6 8PF. Tel: 0115 927 1907.
Westminster, New Road, Sheerness, Kent, ME12 1NB. Fax: 01795
  666606.

Index